D0095019

WHEN
LOVE
ISN'T
EASY

BOOKS BY PHYLLIS HOBE:

Tapestries of Life
The Guideposts Handbook of Prayer
Coping

# WHEN LOVE ISN'T EASY

*Phyllis Hobe*

MACMILLAN PUBLISHING COMPANY

NEW YORK

Copyright © 1985 by Phyllis Hobe

All rights reserved. No part of this book may be reproduced or
transmitted in any form or by any means, electronic or mechanical,
including photocopying, recording, or by any information storage and
retrieval system, without permission in writing from the Publisher.

Macmillan Publishing Company
866 Third Avenue, New York, N.Y. 10022
Collier Macmillan Canada, Inc.

Library of Congress Cataloging in Publication Data
Hobe, Phyllis.
    When love isn't easy.
    1. Love (Theology) 2. Christian life—1960–
I. Title.
BV4639.M57 1985      248.8′43      85-8801
ISBN 0-02-551900-X

Macmillan books are available at special discounts for bulk purchases
for sales promotions, premiums, fund-raising, or educational use.
For details, contact:

Special Sales Director
Macmillan Publishing Company
866 Third Avenue
New York, N.Y. 10022

10 9 8 7 6 5 4 3 2 1

Designed by Jack Meserole

Printed in the United States of America

# Acknowledgments

While writing is admittedly a solitary business, I am always surprised at the number of people who make it possible for me to finish what I set out to do. Many of them don't realize how much help they have given to me, and so I am very pleased that my publishers have allowed me this space in which to tell them.

To Geraldine DePaula, for the gift of listening to an idea as it is newly forming on the tip of the mind; to Lillian Hitt, for communicating her sense of spiritual adventure; to Eleanor Tuttle, whose intelligence, geniality, and exceptional typing skills will never be supplanted by electronic devices; to Jay Acton, for conviction that held even when mine wavered; to friends who put up with my neglect of them for long periods of time, yet never let me forget they were there; to Kate and Mr. Jones, my dog and cat, for their quiet, palpable companionship in the area of my typewriter, not an easy accomplishment when one would rather be playing ball—my gratitude and sincere appreciation for their presence in my life and my work.

# Contents

To Patricia R. Harrington,
whose stubborn encouragement
is a rare kind of love

# Preface

One of the most uncomfortable possibilities confronting women today is that we may not be as loving as we thought we were. This is especially true of women who have already done their share of loving and are finding it too costly to go on. Specifically I am describing the woman whose children are grown but still dependent, whose husband is suffering a midlife crisis, and whose aging parents require the strength and support they once gave to her. Love, at such a time in a woman's life, is difficult. Many of us are finding it impossible.

Some of the most generous mothers I know are struggling with guilt because they resent taking care of children who are old enough to take care of themselves. Some very devoted wives are considering ending a marriage because they feel emotionally abandoned by husbands who are consumed by their own insecurities. Many women are alienated from their aging parents by the shock of seeing them made childlike by the ravages of a long life. And on top of all this is their growing awareness that they, too, were made in the image of God; there is work to be done in their own lives so that the very fact that they were created can mean something. We're all being told now that we can have everything, but we know better. Everything, perhaps, except love, because love takes too much out of us.

It was different when we were younger and loving was easy. When something came over us and made the world and everyone in it seem wonderful. But now we're discovering that the people we loved aren't wonderful. Or perfect. Or problem-free. And we aren't sure we can love them anymore.

It might surprise you to realize that God had the same problem with us after Eden. He didn't like the way we turned out, either. He expected something better, and in His disappointment He tried to turn His back on us. But it didn't work. He evicted us into the world, where death could get at us. At one point we so angered Him that He almost destroyed the earth and us along with it—but not quite. He couldn't, nor could He stop loving us—because love is what He is. So He finally decided to take us back, problems and all. We should understand that because there is something of Him in us, too. And when we don't love, we lose a vital part of ourselves.

Reconciliation wasn't simple for God. He tried to reason with us; He promised not to destroy us, He gave us the earth for a home, He hovered nearby as we groped our way through the world, giving us light when it was dark, food when we could find none, strength against enemies, and all the while assuring us that one day we would be close to Him again. We agreed to His terms—and went on disappointing Him. We weren't the same people He had known in Eden; we had been roughed up by the world, and even though we put up a good front, the absence of God's love had done damage. The easy ways of Eden were outdated, and we needed more than an exchange of promises. We needed a different kind of love; one that was willing to get close enough to be hurt; one that could urge us to try, yet forgive when we failed; one that could find worthy, even delightful, the imperfect fabric of the love we offer in return. We needed the most realistic, most demanding, giving, satisfying, *hardest* love of all. We needed—Jesus Christ.

Very often love is born out of someone's need to be loved, and if we turn away from that need, then we may never experience what love really is. Because love has to be given or it ceases to exist. And how can we—or even God—love unless someone needs what we have to give? That is why love, real love, is never easy. It isn't a response to someone or something wonderful; that's attraction, which is sweet while it lasts. Nor is love something we bestow on those we favor. No. Love is a part of ourselves we yield, often reluctantly, to those who wrench it from us by their need. It is a thoughtful, deliberate, frequently uneven exchange—of appreciation, of problems, of hopes, of disappointments, sometimes of bitter silences or raised voices, and sometimes of sudden, caring intimacies that make us realize how much of life is to be cherished. And in the giving of this love we become more than we were. That is our dividend, often our only one. Yet it is a surprisingly generous one. I know that from my own experience. And from that of many who have loved, perhaps more than I, most lavishly at the very moment when they thought there was no love left in them. Love not only allows us to grow, but makes growing possible.

While it may appear that we women are not as loving as we once were, it is more likely that we are seeking a more realistic kind of love. As we emerge from Eden into the world, we need to experience a love that has nothing to do with our being wonderful, or with someone we love being wonderful, but everything to do with both of us being human. We need to learn how to love in a way that asks nothing in return because, in giving it, we have already gained.

If we are overwhelmed by the needs of others in our life, we have options. We already know we can turn and walk away, leaving part of ourselves with those we once loved. Or we can try to find another Eden where everyone and everything is wonderful until we get to know them better. Or we can do what God chose to do and acknowledge that we need to love others as much as they need our love. We can choose reconciliation, which is really another, perhaps more accurate, word for love.

It will cost us—as it cost God. But we know now that there is more to us than we once believed. We are physically stronger than we supposed. Our minds can search for solutions to the most complex problems. We have the inventive daring of explorers. We can capture the essence of an idea and give it lasting form in words, pictures, music. Even in our later years we have the energy to begin something we thought had passed us by. We may be surprised by such things, but God isn't. He has always known what we are. He has equipped us unstintingly, and we can afford to love. We can't afford not to.

Being a Christian has not brought me peace. It has brought me struggle. It constantly pits my human *no* against God's *yes*, and neither side shows any sign of giving up. Usually my intentions are good, but I don't always follow through on them; God does. I enjoy talking about risks, but I shrink from taking them; God sticks His neck out every time. I'm impatient with errors, especially the same errors committed over and over again; God puts up with them. I hate lies, even my own; somehow God forgives them, even mine. I'm afraid to get hurt—again; so is

God, but He takes the pain. I'm worn out from loving; God always seems to have the energy to try again.

It would be different if God were somewhere out there and I were here. Perhaps I could ignore Him. But our struggle goes on inside me because that is where God is. He's part of me. He wasn't always, but I haven't been the same since it happened. And it happened so simply: I allowed Him to love me.

I used to think it was the other way around, that we were the ones who were supposed to love God. I thought that was what He wanted—no, demanded. I didn't know then what He has always known: that we must first *be* loved before we *can* love. It isn't a matter of following His rules or imitating His example; that would never work. It's a matter of being changed by the experience of being truly loved. That's how and when the struggle begins.

Our capacity to love doesn't increase because God loves us. After all, we're still human beings, and God never intended us to be anything else. But we are no longer able to stop loving. And we look for ways to go on loving even in the most hopeless situations. We aren't left to our own devices anymore; we have God's. Not that we are eager to use them. Oh, no. Who among us wants to take on someone else's resentment, hostility, withdrawal, disregard, deceit, selfishness, and lack of understanding? Especially when there once was love, as we knew it. But that's where the struggle comes in. Because of the God in us we don't live the way we *want;* we live the way we *must.* And there can be no peace, at least not peace as we understood it.

But—"My peace I give unto you: not as the world giveth, give I unto you . . . " Now that's something else again.

WHEN
LOVE
ISN'T
EASY

# 1

## A Person Can Change— Can't She?

BEING WOMEN, we are supposed to know all there is to know about love. And we don't.

Being women, we are said to be able to live for love. We can't. Not anymore.

We know, too, that we don't find anything pleasurable in relationships that give nothing back for all we put into them. Somehow we must find a way to love without being deprived. Or, we must give up loving.

It was much easier for us to love when we could lose ourselves in another person's life. It made us feel that we mattered, and we could understand why God placed so much importance on love. It was beautiful, wonderful, good for us. Thank You, God, for this miracle! And, looking back, it *was* a miracle, because we did things we couldn't possibly do today—knowing what we know now.

We could, for instance, consider it a part of intimacy to put our own needs aside. We could listen endlessly to someone else's concerns and never say a word about our own. We could disguise our disappointment until we forgot we had any. And we could do it all with a smile. Not a phony smile, but a real, deep-down smile that lit up our world in the dark times. We had God and we had love, and we didn't need anything else.

But now we do.

Now it isn't enough to matter to someone else. We know that God took some pains to create us and that we matter, period. We are meant to be more than a part of another's life. We have lives of our own. And yet we're afraid there might be something wrong with the way we feel. We know we are changing, yet we aren't sure we have the right to.

We don't really have any choice. The change is already under way. We notice it in the little things. We're not the good listeners we used to be. Sometimes we don't hear what someone else is saying because another voice is demanding our attention. It sounds like our own. We're becoming more interested in our own thoughts, but we're uncomfortable when they clash with the thoughts of those we love. We try to keep them to ourselves, but they slip out. We never used to be that way. What's happening?

We're growing. The needs that are making us so uncomfortable were there all along, from the moment we took on life. They identify us. They are God's promises to us, and they will continue to unsettle us until we allow God to make good on them.

## The Search for Self

I come from a long line of self-sufficient women. We didn't plan it that way, and we took no particular pride in it. We were just doing what had to be done at the time.

My great-grandmother was widowed when her seven children were quite young, so she went to work as a bookkeeper in her uncle's lumberyard. My grandmother had been a teacher before she married my grandfather, and she stayed on as a substitute because she liked teaching better than housework. She still did her housework, but, according to some people, not too well. She was, they say, an excellent teacher.

My mother always said she had no choice but to work. She blamed it on the Depression, but she kept on working long after the Depression was over. She also did her housework, although my stepfather and I pitched in to help. I was one of very few women in our family to go to college. I went to an all-girls school where the dean used every possible occasion to insist that we could have "husband, home, children—*and* a career." She knew whereof she spoke, because she had done it. Successfully. It was the first time my classmates and I heard anyone say that a woman didn't have to wait for an emergency to discover her abilities. "Learn what they are, develop them—*now!*" our dean said. We were thrilled, and as we looked around us in our all-girls school, we saw our sisters doing a lot of things men ordinarily did. Women put out the newspaper, produced plays, ran for class offices, and were fairly decent athletes. No doubt about it, *we* were going to be something! If our dean could do it, so could we.

Well, we tried to follow the dean's example, but we ran into problems. It seemed impossible to start a family and a career at the same time, so we gave up our plans for a career, or graduate school, or traveling around the world—or whatever it was that once was so important to us. We'd recall our ambitions at class reunions where we'd laugh, not very mirthfully, at what we thought we might have become.

A few of us, and I was one of them, tried to work at a career part-time. But we were defensive about it. We were working to help a husband get started in his career. We were waiting to have children, or, if we had them, a job was something to do while they were in school. Besides, it would help pay for the children's education. Nothing serious, you understand.

It became serious for me when I learned that I probably wasn't going to be a mother, and I decided I had to make some other use of my life. I needed to feel I was worth something. I had wanted a family more than anything in the world, and I was disappointed not to have one. I spent some time being angry with God for not helping me, until I realized that I was behaving like a child who didn't get what she wanted. I began to understand how compassionate God was to lead me in new directions. There were other ways for me to use my talents.

And so I did use them, feeling all along that I had God's support. I did not, however, have the support of a lot of human beings. This happened quite some time ago, and it was unusual for a woman to put as much time into her work as I did. I enjoyed my work, to a degree. I stopped enjoying it at the point where I began to think there was something wrong with me. I used to ask myself how I could leave my husband to fend for himself for as long as a week while I was away on business. For several nights before those trips I would stay up late cooking single-portion meals, which I wrapped in foil, labeled, and froze for him to eat. The poor man felt that if he ate one meal in a restaurant while I was gone, it would be an act of betrayal. And once, when I began to write a list of the order in which he should eat the foil-wrapped meals, he interrupted me. "Please," he said, "let me decide that." I was uncomfortable because my husband rarely had reason to travel by plane, whereas I flew frequently. I worried about a promotion or an increase in salary—Would it make him nervous? Did he secretly resent the fact that he wasn't my whole life? Should he be? Was I doing the wrong thing? Was I less than a real woman?

It bothered me when women—friends of mine—apologized for talking about their children because they thought they were boring me. Or for offering to put a chubby, lovable baby in my arms and then suddenly realizing that chubby, lovable babies can also be very messy and I might not like that. I wouldn't have minded in the least, and I enjoyed talking about children, especially children I particularly liked and would have wanted for my own. It bothered me, too, when my friends whispered to me that I didn't know how lucky I was because they found their lives boring. I didn't think that raising a family ought to be boring; it seemed to require all the intelligence, creativity, inventiveness, courage, good humor, and wit a person might have. I also didn't think my way of life was one long series of adventures; part of it was tedious and run-of-the-mill. The rest of it was demanding and heavy with responsibilities. Besides, I wasn't always certain I was doing the right thing. Life wasn't forcing me to be self-sufficient, as it had my mother, my grandmother, and my great-grandmother. I chose to be that way. And maybe God really wasn't in favor of what I was doing. Maybe I just liked to think He was. If He created women to do more than care for a family, why was I so often the only woman in a conference of men?

I was relieved when more women began to resume or begin careers. I no longer felt out of place. I could share their need to discover what they could accomplish in the world. I knew what it was to swallow hard at the prospect of a challenge and yet to hunger for it. I understood the surprise of finding out how much God had put into me—and how much I could put back into life. But I was disappointed to learn that I was not the only woman who was uncertain about what she was doing. We all were.

It shouldn't have been so surprising.

*God Has a Way of Disrupting Things*

Uncertainty is a part of growing, and we are not the first to be afflicted by it. I doubt that David, when he was herding sheep for a living, ever thought of himself as a king. Nor did the widowed Ruth, scratching in the earth for left-over grain, have any idea that she would enjoy a home and a family again. And Mary, a young girl who knew little about conception except that whatever was happening to her wasn't the way it was supposed to be—hardly what you'd expect of the mother of Christ! Would you ever pick Moses, the abandoned child with the murderous temper, to lead a discontented band of fugitives out of a brutal land? Never! Only God could come up with such possibilities. And such changes.

And what of the people Christ chose to transform a world? They were rough-cut, some of them, barely surviving with crude skills passed down to them by generations who had done no better. Some were more educated, perhaps, but not entirely upright when it came to the law. Some, with more than enough for themselves, were not above taking from the smaller stores of those less fortunate. Not all of them men, either. A prostitute, accustomed to speaking to men in whispered invitations, threw herself at His feet and wept with joy, calling Him God out loud. A businesswoman (yes, there were a few then, too), farm women, wives, mothers, all of them leaving the shelter of life's fringes to be where He was, even if it meant danger. A very uncertain group.

Like us, probably none of them would have chosen to change. At first they may have been dazzled by the possibilities Christ found in them. But they, too, had families, friends, old relationships, and responsibilities that would be affected by the change. We can imagine how a fisher-man's wife must have felt when her husband put aside his nets and went off to become a "fisher of men." We can sympathize with the panic of an aging woman when her sons, her only means of support, left her to follow a Man with no money of His own. She could hardly have thought her sons were improving their lot. Or hers.

Achieving our potential can be very hard on those we love. And on us.

There are times when I wish I could just be left alone to do what I have to do and be what I want to be. It's not that I want to abandon the people I care about, but I need time to myself, a part of the world I can call my own. I don't think I'm the only woman who has this need. And I don't think I'm the only one who feels she has to apologize for it.

Recently I was talking to a friend who has been a widow for several years and is planning to remarry. While she looks forward to sharing her life again, she is also a bit ap-prehensive about it. "When you live alone for a while," she said, "you get used to doing things your way." I under-stood.

"I don't know if I'm fit for marriage anymore," she said, laughing. "I don't want to stop being who I am." There—it slipped out, and we both realized there wasn't anything funny about what she said. We tried to change the subject after that, but couldn't. We ran out of talk and lost ourselves in our thoughts, which I'm sure were a lot alike.

What we both meant, and didn't want to put into words, was: Can we be ourselves and still be what other people want us to be? It's a question many women are ask-ing, and most of them aren't living alone. Yet. They're liv-ing in couples and in families, and they're wondering whether the good thing that has happened to them is going to spell the end of the other good things in their lives. Or, they're wondering whether the thing that has happened to them is any good at all. There is a Martha and a Mary in us, and they set us at war within ourselves. Sometimes we feel like Martha, grumbling in the kitchen, but not sure of our ability to keep up with what is going on outside it. We hear Christ calling to us to come and be builders of His world as well as its caretakers. The Mary in us wants to get cracking, but the Martha wonders if we have what it takes to get on in the world. Well, we can't know, for sure. We have His word for what we are worth, and not everyone we know agrees with Him.

## If We Feel Uncertain . . .

It's understandable. We have never been where we are about to go. No mothers, aunts, grandmothers, or favorite teachers, now retired, can tell us what it will be like to complete ourselves—they haven't been there. Not quite. We can't follow in anyone's footsteps because there aren't any. Each of us is taking an unmarked trail, and parts of it will be thick with underbrush. We may have to slow down to clear some of it out of our way. Much of the going will be uphill, and we will have to stop for breath. It will be a long time before we reach a place where we can get a clear view of what is behind and what lies ahead. None of us has gone that far. We have to proceed on faith.

And whoever said that faith was a sure thing? Far from it. When the Son of God walked among us as a Man of flesh and blood, it wasn't easy to believe. Now we are trying to become the persons God originally meant us to be. We can't see these selves or touch them, but we know they exist. We have that faith—most of the time. It's when we, or someone else, notices something different about us that our faith falters. We can't prove what we believe to be true, and suddenly we wonder, "*Is* it true?" Faith is like that. So is God. Such things can only be seen with eyes grown accustomed to the flickering nature of spiritual light. It will be a while before we have such vision. When we do, we will know that in between the times of brightness there are moments of darkness when we aren't certain that we are going in the right direction. But the moments of darkness don't last.

## If We Feel Guilty . . .

We have our reasons. It isn't easy to do what someone you love doesn't like. Sometimes not even a word has to be said—you can see it in a glance, or in a turning away of the eyes. And you feel you have done something wrong. The truth is that you have, but it started a long time ago. And while you are not to blame, you *are* responsible. You asked someone else—not God—to create you.

We all do it. We begin when we are very young, when we aren't clearly defined. *We* don't know who we are, so how can anyone else, except God? But we don't ask God who we are; we ask someone close to us. And the way we ask is so simple: *Do you love me?* Depending on the answer, we either change what we are—or we don't dare to change a thing. Of course we don't ask the question outright. We rephrase it, depending upon the person we want to define us. But the meaning remains the same.

We begin with our parents: *Who can I be to make you proud of me?*

Then our friends: *What kind of a person can you be close to?*

Perhaps a teacher: *How can I make you feel that you have accomplished something?*

Or someone we love: *How can I thank you for finding me?*

A partner in life: *How can I hold onto you?*

And if we have children: *What will make you remember me?*

But there is this, too: *I will give up, or add to, whatever I become to please you. I am the most adjustable being you have ever known. All you have to do is tell me that you love me and I will become whatever you can love.*

Gradually we acquire an identity: We are what someone else wants us to be. And that can be wonderful—except when it comes into conflict with what another Someone wants us to be. It's happening to us now. We are caught between being created by God and being created by those we have loved. We don't fit as snugly into other people's lives, but, then, we aren't meant to. We need room to become more than we are, and in the process of growing we will rub against one another.

We aren't the only ones who are changing. We are discovering strengths we never knew we had, but men are learning that strength is not all they are. There is a gentle side to men, which must be explored, and they are struggling to understand its unfamiliar ways. While we are delighted to find we are younger than we thought, our children feel very old for this world. They are shocked by the aggressiveness the world requires of them; they expected to live more peaceably, and they need time to make the adjustment. We can hope to live many more years, so we dare to start life over at fifty or later, but our parents are finding their added years a mixed blessing. They didn't know they would have to worry about money and sickness and loneliness and boredom. They thought such things were behind them.

All of us are becoming sensitive to new talents that insist on being used, new needs that, unless satisfied, will keep us awake in the night searching the darkness for some explanation of our restlessness. Like us, the ones we love are caught in a turmoil that both excites and terrifies them in the same moment. We know what we are, yet God has given us a glimpse of what we might become. In this shifting middle ground there is tension, fear of the unknown and the awful possibility that we might be wrong, that we might not be able to live up to God's expectations. His promises are beautiful, but we don't know if we will like the kind of life that goes with them.

There again we have no choice. Our lives are changing because our world is changing, and God has given us the ability to meet its new demands.

We welcome the light of day and can't imagine a world without it, yet when the sun first pushed back the darkness, the effect must have been alarming. And quite possibly the darkness, if it could have made its feelings known, didn't relish sharing the earth with it. Plant life disrupts the soil and, if not restrained, will exhaust it. Life of any kind—plant, animal, and especially human—rearranges the face of the earth and all that goes on in it. Yet, without change, without growth, life can't continue.

Jesus Christ was the most challenging call to change that the world has known. Consider how men and women must have felt when they were told that God had sent His own Son to be with them. Consider being in His presence, experiencing the warm, palpable press of His most human hand as He spoke of a spiritual Father's love for each of His utterly human children. More than that—consider hearing Him say that He would, in His human form, take our place in a confrontation with death. He would do the dying for us.

Our job, now, is to do the living for Him. And we find that hard—because it *is* hard. He knows that.

Still, there are those lingering questions . . .

*How Can We Be Sure We're Becoming What God Wants Us to Be?*

We can't. Not any of us. Ever.

I have wasted a lot of time waiting for God to tell me what to do. And God has wasted a lot of good advice on me because I didn't recognize it when I got it. I expected guidance to come in a more dramatic form. An order, perhaps, or a command, something I couldn't possibly ignore or avoid. It's so much easier to be told what to do than to make up your own mind. But most of the time God guides us in subtle ways. He gave us the ability to make our own decisions and He expects us to use it.

He can move mountains, and He has moved some that I put there in the first place. He has even dropped a few mountains right in my path because that was the only way He could stop me. But I can't count on Him to step in and restore order everytime I create chaos. He will not allow me to become His puppet.

What I can count on is that God is with me in whatever I choose to do. If I manage to do what is best for me, I can sense not only His pleasure, but His relief. If I take the wrong turn, He takes it with me. When I can't find my way, He throws some light on the path so that I can muddle through or get back to where I started. If I fall, and I often do, He falls with me and, believe me, He feels the impact more than I do. (That's what happens when you love someone.)

I used to think that if God wanted me to achieve something, He would make it possible. And if He didn't like what I was trying to do, He would see to it that I failed. I was wrong. I have succeeded in achieving some goals that weren't worth the effort I put into reaching them. I have also found it difficult to reach some goals that turned out to be the best things in the world for me. So the ease or the hardship of my life doesn't tell me whether I am doing what God wants me to do. God tells me—*if* I pay attention. Not to what is going on outside, but to what is going on inside me. Because that is where God is, and He does not leave, not for a second. He does give me advice and quite specific guidance, but in quiet ways I can choose to ignore— and unfortunately sometimes I do.

Ever since I was a child, I have been trying *not* to be a writer. Yet ever since I was a child, I have had a compulsion to put my thoughts and feelings into words. Written words. There was something special about the way a pencil, and later a pen, felt in my hand. I never became a good typist, but as I strike the keys, forming words from the bits and pieces of ideas that had no shape before, something in me comes together, too. I feel whole. And there is very little in the world that can unsettle my life at such times.

But I didn't think I wanted to be a writer because it didn't fit in with the way I was brought up. My family valued security. They were willing to work hard and devotedly, but they needed the assurance that there would always be work for them to do. They were comfortable with schedules, procedures, and regular hours. The life and the working habits of a writer seemed irresponsible to them and, consequently, to me.

For many years I tried to divide my working life. I spent most of it in the business world and wrote when I had the time, which wasn't often. While I didn't do too badly in a business environment, I wasn't comfortable there. I was always trying to change things, always looking for new ways to accomplish what I wanted to do, and very impatient with the need to persuade others to go along with me.

As you can imagine, I was often frustrated, and I blamed it on my lack of discipline.

Curiously, when I worked as a writer, I was a highly disciplined person. I had no problem working alone. Because my own schedule made sense to me, I valued it and stuck to it. I never felt as if the world had forgotten me if the phone didn't ring; I could even ignore the ringing phone if I had a deadline to meet. I never raided the refrigerator or looked for reasons to avoid my typewriter. In fact, I lived a well-regulated life, which is exactly what my family had been doing for generations. The only difference was that I was a writer. If I wanted security, and I did, then I had to find something to write that someone wanted to read. If I needed to know that there was more work for me to do, and I did, then I had to work hard and devotedly as my family had always done.

Eventually the opportunities for me to write came more often, which forced me to make a decision. Now I could say that this was God's way of telling me to be a writer, but I don't think it was. I simply functioned more effectively when I used the abilities God gave me—instead of trying to do what others before me had done so well.

I know now that God does not impose His will on us at certain times in our lives. It is always with us, just as He is always with us. Nor does His will mean that we should do—or not do—such-and-such. His will is that we should become what He created us to be, and that is not a simple matter for Him to make known to us. Our own impulses keep getting in the way.

It took time for me to realize that, whichever way I chose to go, God would not abandon me. Nor would He punish me if He didn't agree with my choice. He would stay with me and help me over the rough spots. But I would be far better equipped for my journey if I used what He had given to me. At that point the choice became obvious. I was a writer.

The journey hasn't been easier; at times it is more difficult, because it means more to me. But I am better suited to what I am doing. I think I am more effective in the world, and this is what God intends for me. I have that feeling of coming together, of being whole, much more often, and I understand why. I am, much more often, doing what God already knows is best for me. And by that I don't mean that everything in my life is orderly, because it isn't. But I can deal with the disorder, I can live with what is not as I would wish it to be. I am not distracted by such things as I once was. The feeling of wholeness is my coming together with God. I am taking my place not only as a sharer in His world, but as one of its builders, and that is what He has in mind for each of us. We are here to change this world, not to our specifications, but to His. First, however, we have to change ourselves.

## Are We Selfish to Pay Attention to Our Own Needs?

Were the disciples? Were they selfish to grow beyond their immediate appetites?

In their early days of following a Man some thought was a king, they surely must have had expectations of a better way of life. After all, they were associates of Someone who drew crowds in the street. They had seen Him change water into wine, cause the blind to see, and order the lame to walk. With their own eyes they had witnessed Him bring the dead back to life. Surely He could bring them comfort, ease, perhaps even affluence. He spoke of mansions, a kingdom, and while they didn't understand what He meant by such words, they must have hoped that they would share in the benefits of such a realm. He had singled them out. He saw something of value in them—and if they couldn't see it, what difference did it make? This most amazing Man was pleased with them—and He would reward them.

We are not any different from those dearly human persons. We confuse our appetites with our needs. We hunger for something and give our lives over to its pursuit, and if we don't get what we seek, we count our lives poorly spent. But a need is not a hunger; it will be activated rather than satisfied by being fed. A need is a hand seeking work to do and a tool to do it with; it is Michelangelo demanding sharp chisels to wield against an exquisite block of marble so that some sense can be made out of it. A hunger seeks to be quieted; a need must be expressed.

Christ ignored hungers, but paid great attention to needs. He could urge us not to worry about how we were going to pay for our next meal, yet He could look into our eyes and find some substance there.

We are not wrong to want some security in life. We are not God, and we can't see beyond the next obstacle or threat to our existence. Our hungers are of use in many ways, and I am not alone in recalling the worthwhile things I have done out of necessity. But security and the calming of an appetite are not my needs.

If you ask me what my needs are, I may not be able to tell you, but I can feel them within me. They do not make me comfortable. I am like a disciple who looks forward to a piece of a kingdom and then finds myself left with work to do in it. I am incomplete, and my needs tell me what I must have to become competent.

Why *competent?*

Because—again, like the disciples—I am finding that what I have been given is not mine to hold. There is a kingdom, yes. And it requires my participation. It needs what God has given me and trusts me to bring to completion. So if *I* have needs, they are not mine alone—they are God's as well.

## Do We Have to Change?

We will change, all of us, whether we consent to it or not. Change is a part of our development, just as aging is a part of growth. If we oppose making the best use of what God has given us, then our lives will be changed by those who reach out for the blessing, and whose relationship to us will thereby be changed. Because blessings, like creativity itself, are explosive. If one of us grows, everyone that person knows will be affected by it.

I can't hold you back if you become more completely yourself. But I can blame you for being different from the person I used to know. I can accuse you of giving more attention to yourself than to me. I can cry out that since I have adapted myself to what you were, you owe me your continuance as that person. I can plead with you not to leave me, when in truth you are simply walking at your own pace while I remain rooted in one spot.

I don't have to keep up with you. Or follow the same route. But I do have to honor my own needs. That is the only way I can understand yours.

## How Can We Go On Loving?

We aren't meant to stop loving, but to learn how. There is a way of caring that allows us to look after the needs of others as well as our own. There is a way to help another person find his or her identity—without giving up our own. It is not the way we have been loving each other. It is the way God loves us. And, like the relationship between God and us, it is not without difficulties.

Love is not a service we perform for someone important to us. It does not pick up after loved ones, nor does it pack lunches, run errands, do laundry, and take the car to be repaired. It does not sit up in a darkened room anxiously pressing a hand to a feverish head. It does not greet loved ones cheerfully even if it is not cheerful. It does not listen patiently to the same stories it has heard so many times before. It does not try to stay young, or keep romance alive, or bite its lip to keep from crying because its efforts are not appreciated. Or even noticed. Love is none of these things. We only thought it was, because we never took a good look at it.

Love is not an exchange of sentiment, of emotions, of best wishes on carefully chosen greeting cards. It is an exchange of creative power; it is giving to each other the courage to get from where we are to where God wants us to be. It is constantly changing, constantly growing, always disrupting. It is the impact of God upon human life, and if we are going to love, then we had better expect to be shaken up. It's push comes to shove all the way.

I remember being considered "agreeable" as a child, and I enjoyed that reputation. I didn't go out of my way to seek anyone's favor, but I could be reasoned with and rarely lost my temper. I also liked being likable.

One of my favorite people was my Aunt Vera, my father's younger sister. She was pretty and much more fun than any of the other grown-ups I knew. On Saturdays she used to call for me and take me shopping with her, and I was proud that she preferred my company.

We always ended our day with a visit to the five-and-ten, where I was allowed to choose one small toy to take home with me. I looked forward to Saturdays generally, but going to the five-and-ten was the best part. Aunt Vera liked to laugh, and she was like a little girl herself as she picked up a ball, a card of jacks, a cellophane-wrapped doll's dress, a book of paper dolls, a bubble pipe, holding up each one for my approval.

I don't know what got into me, but on one Saturday the toy section of the five-and-ten lost its magic. I didn't want anything Aunt Vera offered me. I kept pulling her over to the gardening counter. I didn't want a toy. I wanted a package of seeds. It was spring, and I wanted to grow flowers. Aunt Vera thought that was silly, since I lived in an apartment and didn't have a garden. She took me right back to the toys, where there was still plenty of magic for her. She paid no attention to my insistence that if she would only buy me a package of seeds, I would find a place to plant them. I still remember feeling as if I had been put in a wooden box and was trying to pound my way out of it. Finally I went into a rage. I refused to let Aunt Vera take my hand. I told her—screamed it, actually—that she was mean. If I couldn't have the seeds, I didn't want anything. I didn't ever want to go shopping with her again. I *hated* her!

And I will never, ever forget the look on Aunt Vera's face. She was so hurt that it frightened me into silence.

On the train going home we found seats together, but we sat inches apart, saying nothing to each other. I was stunned by what I had done. Young as I was, I realized I had hurt someone I loved, someone who loved me dearly, and I was in mourning. Did a package of seeds mean that much to me?

Actually it did—not the seeds, but what they symbolized. I was growing up, a little. New interests were vying with old ones for my attention. Suddenly I saw more than toys in the five-and-ten, and I wanted to do more than play. I was becoming aware of something that is very important in my life now: I love to grow flowers.

Of course, going back home with Aunt Vera that Saturday, I didn't know any of this. Neither did Aunt Vera. We only knew that we didn't seem like the same persons to each other, and that we never would again. Growing up excited me; it frightened Aunt Vera, and she wanted to postpone it for as long as she could.

As the numbness of my bewilderment began to wear off, I realized that I still loved my Aunt Vera. I felt so relieved that I started to cry. I tried to do it quietly, but Aunt Vera saw what was going on. She put her arm around me and pulled me close to her. Her face, next to mine, was wet with tears, too: her own. We both were groping for new ways to love each other. We could go on being playmates, but we would have to learn how to accommodate the differences in each of us.

We continued to go shopping on Saturdays, but we avoided the five-and-ten. Aunt Vera took me to the movies instead, always to movies appropriate for children, and she seemed to enjoy them as much as I did. Never again did she attempt to hold me back from growing up, and I tried not to pull her along with me. Somehow we managed to remain each other's favorite person.

When I was in college, struggling with a heavy schedule and a job that wasn't paying me as much as I needed, Aunt Vera was the only person I could tell my troubles to. I wondered why at the time. Friends and other family members would have been sympathetic, but for them I put on a smile. For them I pretended to be the capable adult, although I felt like a frightened child. When I wrote to Aunt Vera, I didn't have to pretend. I wept. And when her letters arrived, I giggled. They were always several pages long, filled with sound advice in her graceful handwriting. And right in the middle of sentences and all over the margins were dimple-kneed, rascally-eyed, pen-drawn figures of little girls having the most outrageous fun—chasing balls, skipping rope, eating Popsicles, holding worn-out Teddy bears behind their backs, feeding birds, petting kittens, and generally finding the world a good place to be. The child in Aunt Vera was reminding me that there was a child in me, too, and that I needed her. She could help me to see that sometimes we adults take things too seriously.

I truly believe that the little girl in Aunt Vera got me through college, and I am very grateful that she was not entirely lost when Aunt Vera finally decided, as we all must, that it was time to put aside childish things.

Aunt Vera and I were a success story. I can't say as much for some other encounters I have had with people who didn't want me to change. Too often I reacted harshly, and it made me feel wrong. Yet I *was* wrong. Not wrong to grow, not wrong to want to learn more about the self I was created to be. But wrong to react so bitterly when someone tried to hold me back. A few times, to avoid the sickening feeling of being wrong, I tried not to change. Not to grow. And that was worse, because I still felt wrong, but for different reasons: I was unfair to myself, I was ignoring God, and I blamed the person I loved for my unhappiness. Add up a few more incidents of that kind and I was back in a wooden box, trying to pound my way out. If I didn't scream "I hate you!" to someone I loved, I certainly meant it. The message got through anyway, and that was the end of love. Neither I nor the person I had loved could do what Aunt Vera had done, which was to take the first step toward the other. She did it with a hug, a simple gesture I could not make. Not when someone had let me down.

But then, Aunt Vera had help, as I realized many years later. She may have grown up as a person, but she never stopped being a child of God, and she trusted Him to help her live in this world. Perhaps that explains why she was a happy person in spite of the fact that she had an unhappy life. She married a dear and delightful man who was a dreamer, and as one dream after another dissolved before their eyes, they found it hard to make ends meet. She had several children; some of them turned out well, and a few not so well. But she loved them all, especially the youngest, who had had a difficult birth and died at the age of three. When friends, trying to console her, reminded her that she had other children, she would simply say, "But I loved him, too."

I learned of these things long after Aunt Vera died because when I finished college, we lost touch with each other. Or, rather, I lost touch with her. That's a long story, which I'll try to shorten.

I asked Aunt Vera to help me get in touch with my father, who was divorced from my mother when I was two and hadn't seen me in all those years. And, of course, Aunt Vera said yes. My father and I met at her house, and we spent a wonderful afternoon thinking we were getting to know each other, which was not what was happening. The reality of the situation was far more complicated. My father had married again and had another family, who were not, understandably, at ease with my sudden reappearance. I was grown and married, not at all the infant my father remembered. My mother had tried to be both parents to me, which was impossible, and I had a stepfather who knew me better than my father did. I was a stranger, asking for a father's love. I can't say that either one of us was right or wrong, but I can tell you it was impossible for us to meet again, being the persons we were. Too many others whom we loved would have been hurt. We were not wise enough to handle the changes that would come into our lives. And, unlike Aunt Vera, we didn't ask God to help. I can't speak for my father, but as far as I was concerned, I thought we were caught in a knot made by some very foolish people and I didn't think it was fair to ask God to untangle it.

So, when my father decided that it would be best for us to forget about each other, I was hurt. And bitter. I thought I could cry on Aunt Vera's shoulder, but that wasn't what happened. She knew I was hurt, and she comforted me. But she didn't go along with my bitterness. "Your father has a lot of problems, and I think you ought to take that into consideration," she said. I couldn't do that, and I accused Aunt Vera of taking sides. I kept my distance from her after that and never gave her a chance to hug me again. I wanted her to be wrong.

I know now that she wasn't.

I might still have a hard time trying to understand my father even now, but I think I am beginning to love him. It isn't easy. And it isn't something I can do on my own. But I think I am beginning to realize what my Aunt Vera must have known at a much earlier age. That love is never easy. And that we must get help from God. Because He's the One who started it in the first place.

# 2

## Nobody's Easy to Love

IT HAS TAKEN ME more years than I care to count to learn that I never really knew most of the persons I have loved. I never really loved them, either. I wanted to, and I thought I did. But I didn't understand what love was, and even if I had, I don't think I could have handled it. I had a lot of growing to do first.

I remember the very moment when I realized that my mother was not the most beautiful woman in the world. I don't know why it is, but little girls—and perhaps little boys, too—have to believe that their mother is the best of all persons. And the best, to me, included being the most beautiful. My mother was an attractive woman, pretty, and she dressed with taste. I'm sure it pleased her to have me think she was beautiful, but I doubt she ever knew how important it was to me to believe she was more beautiful than any other woman. By loving her, I was making her beauty mine. Love was my way of becoming part of someone wonderful. And that made me wonderful, too.

But I was getting older, and certain bits of reality were forcing themselves into my life. My mother and I were on a bus one day, standing in the aisle because there were no seats available. I looked down at a woman seated in front of me, and I couldn't deny that she was beautiful. That upset me. In my mind I began arguing with myself, insisting that my mother was more beautiful. But I looked at my mother and again at the woman, and I felt sad and angry at the same time. Sad that a myth had died, and angry at my mother for not living up to my expectations. At that moment, I did not love my mother—because she stopped being wonderful, and so did I.

Now, many years later, if you were to ask me how I feel about my mother, I would tell you that I love her very much, even though I know she is not wonderful at all. And neither am I. In fact, my mother is a disturbed, tormented person who makes it hard for anyone, including herself, to love her. Yet I can love many things about her that she herself doesn't value or realize she has. My mother has had little formal education, but she has a passion for learning. She reads more than anyone I know. By the next day she may have forgotten what she read, but that doesn't matter. She goes on reading because she has a hunger to understand. She couldn't tell you what she wants to understand, because that is part of her search. But the searching and the hunger and the passion to learn are what I love. She was able to recognize a similar hunger in me and she taught me to read and write long before I was old enough to go to school. She worked all day at a demanding job, so it wasn't easy for her to spend her evenings teaching a little girl to connect carefully drawn letters and to sound out words. But somehow she had the patience for it.

My mother demands a great deal of attention, more than anyone can satisfy, which makes loving her very frustrating. But she also senses when other people need to know they are important. Whenever I had a part in a school program, she was always in the audience, even though it

meant taking time off from her job and traveling quite far
each way by bus. Later on she might find fault with my
performance and tell me someone else had done better, and
that was hard for me to take. But now I can look back and
understand that her presence in a front row was her way of
telling me I was important to her. At the time I wanted
more than her presence, but, you see, that's what I mean
when I say I didn't really know the person I loved. I didn't
recognize the fact that my mother couldn't give me what I
wanted. And to stop loving her for that reason was as foolish as to love her because I thought she was the most beautiful woman in the world.

We cannot ever love people for what we think they are
or might become. We can only try to love them for what we
know they are, and in the harsh glare of what we see very
clearly they are not. It is easy to love a myth of our own
making. It allows us to remain a myth to ourselves as well.
Then, when the one we love develops signs of being all too
human, we can walk away angrily and look for another
myth. In the meantime we remain lost to ourselves and we
wonder why God insists that we love one another. After a
few attempts, we come to the conclusion that it's down-
right impossible.

And it is—unless we become real to ourselves and to
each other. That may be one of the most vital messages
Christ brought us when He came among us as a human
being. I am real, He may have been saying, as you are real.
And love, too, is real.

Now—what does that have to do with real life?

### Instead of Love

For several years I knew them as a special family who, in
the words of one of them, "had a lot of love going on." Ev

and Sally, the parents, were the kind of people other people liked to be with: attractive, intelligent, devoted to each other, energetic. Their children, Sue and Dave, fit in beautifully: healthy, good grades, lots of friends, bright but not too bright, easygoing but not drifting. Ev was the evident head of the family, but Sally didn't give in easily; she had spunk. Sue took after her; and Dave, well, he was steady, like his dad.

Ev had a good job and was respected in his field. He could afford to give his family a comfortable life: a charming house on the fringes of the city, good schools for the kids, a tennis club for Ev and Sally, not a lot of clothes, but good ones, a respectable car, and a growing nest of investments. The future was promising. Ev was slated to become a company vice-president; he had built his life around that goal.

There were a few shadowy areas in the family picture. The harder Ev worked and the more he was praised by his bosses, the more he pushed and the more he worried—late at night, sometimes, when he thought Sally was asleep and didn't hear him padding downstairs for a glass of milk with a shot of bourbon in it to calm him down. And Sally had those times when she cried for no reason at all and couldn't stop. But she always did it alone. Sue and Dave were teenagers, so you never could tell what they'd do next. Except that they weren't doing anything out of the ordinary. They were too quiet, almost as though they were afraid to do something wrong. Nevertheless, nobody paid attention to those little problems. After all, they were a special family, with a "lot of love going on."

It all happened quickly, one thing after another.

Ev's company was bought out by a competitor and he lost his job.

Sally went into the guest room up in the attic and wouldn't come out.

Dave dropped out of his first year of college and took odd jobs. He told his father he wanted to "find himself."

And Sue? She didn't say much, but she transferred to a college near home so she could commute. She was losing a lot of weight, which wasn't necessarily a sign of trouble. She had been overweight all through high school.

Eventually they had to sell the house. But that wasn't the worst of it. Everything they loved about each other was gone. Ev wasn't the steady, sturdy man Sally used to depend on. He was scared. He needed Sally's strength, and both of them were horrified to find that she didn't have much to give. Even in the best of times, Sally wasn't sure of herself, but there had always been Ev to hide behind. Neither one of them could face the possibility that their children were having problems, so they ignored them—and the children *knew* they were being ignored.

At Ev's age, it wasn't easy to find another job, but finally he did. The company was smaller, so was the salary, and Ev worried more than ever about his future. "But, there's only me now," he said. He meant that his family was gone. One day Sally had come down from the attic and asked for a divorce. "She told me she didn't love me anymore," Ev said. The children? He saw them now and then. "I guess we all stopped loving each other," he said. "Those things happen."

No, they don't.

We don't *stop* loving. But all too often we never begin. We do something else instead: We admire. We create in each other what we think is missing in ourselves. And that isn't real.

Ev's steadiness, Sally's cheerleader breeziness, the children's unprotesting obedience, all these qualities were admirable. The trouble was, they didn't exist. Ev was an uncertain man. He had trouble believing he was as capable as everyone, including himself, claimed he was. But he couldn't very well admit it. Who would love such a man? Certainly not a woman like Sally, who was exactly the kind of wife Ev always wanted. A confident woman with a twinkle in her eye. A woman who expected success and knew how to enjoy it. Ev wouldn't have believed it if he knew how Sally felt about herself—that she was a born failure, that no matter what she tried to do with her life, the answer always would be the same: that she wasn't good enough; that what she needed was a successful man like Ev to take care of her.

Sue and Dave didn't have a chance. Sure, they were model kids; that's where the love was. But sometimes they used to envy their parents for being so self-confident. Sue and Dave didn't feel that way at all, but they thought they were wrong to have doubts about themselves.

Suddenly, in this family where there was "a lot of love going on," no one could give anything to another. Because there was nothing left to admire. There were only the things they didn't want in one another, or in themselves—the weaknesses and the dependencies, the fears and the big talk to drown out the fears, the accusations and the resentments. They had never discovered so many other valuable qualities that lay, undetected and never used, beneath what they wanted one another to be. And so they never were able to give one another, or themselves, what they really needed: understanding, compassion, comfort, support, sensitivity. But, then, who needs such things?

We all do.

Because without them we aren't real, not to ourselves

nor to anyone else. They are our means of communication, the channels through which we identify ourselves to those we love.

## All Right, Then, What Is Real?

Real leaves nothing out. When it comes to love, it means we don't invent each other. We give each other not only the best that we are, but the worst, and everything in between. It also means we take our chances on what we might become, because we know we're going to change.

Sounds risky, doesn't it? It is.

We don't even like everything about ourselves. So how can we possibly like everything about someone else?

We can't.

Love doesn't always like. It doesn't excuse, it doesn't overlook, but it does embrace the whole person. It cares. Love can wash the road-weary feet of loved ones while they complain that they aren't loved enough. Love can take upon its own body the wounds meant for those it loves while those it loves keep a safe distance.

Impossible, you say. You're quite right. This is not our kind of love. It is God's. We love each other the way we love ourselves, admiringly, unrealistically, which is not the way God loves us. And therein lies our problem. Because we cannot really love each other until we learn what it is to *be* loved.

My own capacity to love is very brief. It depends a great deal upon the person I love and how wonderful that person appears to be. It depends, also, upon what I expect that person to accomplish. And—I admit, reluctantly—upon what that person's accomplishments bring to my life. I'm not talking about material well-being, and I would be embarrassed at the possibility that I might expect some sort of

tangible gain out of loving. But I do require a certain emo-
tional dividend from the persons I love. Specifically I
require them to live up to my belief that they are—
magnificent. You see, I want my love to be deserved. I want
it to reflect back on my own good taste in choosing someone worthy of being loved.

Now—can you see why I am often disappointed by the
ones I love? Or—are you too painfully close to disappointment of your own?

My kind of love—and it is your kind, too, because it is
human—cannot last long. It begins to come apart at the first
sign of trouble. And by that I intend no criticism. You and I
do the best we can. We give all the love we have. But we're
afraid we don't have much to give, so we want to get something back for what we give. After all, we need love, too!

Correction: The truth is, we need love—first. We have to
learn how to value ourselves before we can understand the
value of others.

## How Do I Love Me?

The hardest person in the world to love is oneself. This
is what gets in the way of our loving others. No one has to
tell me about my faults. I have plenty of them. Therefore I
find it hard to love the person I am.

I also find it hard to love God, but for totally different
reasons. He *is* perfect. Yet He loves me—and I can't understand why. Or how.

Now—why can't I love God in spite of the fact that I
don't love myself? Because, to me, love has to work both
ways. I can't expect you to love me unless I am lovable.
And if I don't think that I am, then I'm not going to believe
you when you tell me you love me. After all, we don't get
something for nothing.

Oh, yes, we do, because that's what love is: something for nothing.

And we don't know how to love that way, because it isn't natural to us. We have to learn it from God.

## Teach Me

Some years ago I went into business with three people I loved, admired, and respected, and they felt the same way about me. Working together was a joy—until the stress of trying to do too much in a short time got to us. We were working on a shoestring, as far as money was concerned, so if one of us made a mistake or missed a deadline, we all felt the results in our income. We were quick to blame one another. We became so afraid of failing that we couldn't possibly survive, and the quality of our work was affected. Finally we had the good sense to call it quits before we got into debt. But our friendship—the love, admiration, and respect we used to feel for one another—ended when our little business did. It could not endure what we did not like in one another.

To me the loss was especially devastating because I had recently lost two other people who were close to me. One had died, and another, a friend for many years, moved away. I had other friends, but I didn't want to see them. I couldn't explain why, not even to myself. I only knew that I felt totally cut off from everyone. I couldn't ignore the fact that I wasn't being loved by some people I wanted to love, and for some reason I just couldn't love at all. I never felt so isolated in my life. I was suffering from an affliction that strikes us all at one time or another: I was mad at the world.

I thought I had a good relationship with God. He had helped me through some difficult times I couldn't have handled on my own. So I believed that He loved me. But then I asked myself, How could I be sure He did? If God loved me, how could He let me suffer so many losses? Why didn't He help me find ways to hold onto people I loved? Didn't he care that I was unhappy? And if He really loved me, why didn't I *feel* loved?

Late on a rainy summer afternoon I came home after being away for two days. I had boarded my dog and cat, so there was no one to welcome me, and in the mood I was in, I felt that even my house was rejecting me. The lock wouldn't give way to my key for the longest time, and the door stuck. The heat and humidity had a lot to do with my difficulties, but I didn't see it that way.

I had used up all of my self-control during the ups and downs of the past few months. I had bitten bullets and made hard decisions because there was nothing else I could do. No tears, no angry outbursts—what could they accomplish? But when my house seemed to be trying to keep me out, I couldn't take it. As the tumbler finally yielded to my key, I threw myself against the swollen door and fell inside as it opened.

My knee hurt, and in anger I kicked at the door with my foot, missing it entirely. Embarrassed by my childish behavior I got up from the floor, carried my luggage inside and somehow found the patience to close and lock the resisting door. Then I tried to carry everything upstairs in one trip and I stumbled. I bumped my shin hard against a stair.

"What are you trying to do?" I cried out. "Get even with yourself?"

For what? I hadn't done anything.

Oh, yes, I had. I had lost love, and none of us has much to spare. Obviously I was more angry at myself than at the world, and I was trying to get even with myself for becoming someone no one, not even God, could love.

But then God corrected me.

It happened quietly, slowly. No big spiritual hug. No

"There, there, you'll be all right." Just a gradual clearing in my mind, a pushing back of the unkindnesses I had hurled at myself. And into that area of serenity came remembered faces of the friends I hadn't wanted to see because I thought I had lost the ability to love them. But I *wasn't* loving them then; they were loving *me*. I was recalling their little acts of caring and small gestures of understanding, some of them going back many years. I had been so busy trying to earn their admiration that I had overlooked their offerings of love.

I believed then, and I believe it now, that God was teaching me, in very human terms, how it feels to *be* loved. It's what we all have to learn before we *can* love.

## Love Gives Me Its Attention

Even when there is something else on His mind, God listens to me whenever I need to talk to Him. I know I don't always make sense to Him, but that isn't what matters. At times I come close to exhausting His patience, especially when I ask for His advice and then I don't use it. I can arouse His anger by crying about a mistake I've made many times already and still haven't learned anything from it. But He hears me. Always.

He also knows what I am doing. In spite of all the other lives that share His attention, He never takes His mind off me. The very fact that I exist affects the way He thinks and what He does. My being is important to Him.

He doesn't look over my shoulder. He doesn't pry. He is aware of me. He doesn't ask me where I'm going and how long I'll be there. He knows I can look after myself. But He can hear the cry I cannot utter. He smiles when I laugh. He frowns when I take on something bigger than I am, but He keeps His distance as long as I can handle it. And when all is well with me, and sometimes that happens, I can almost feel His relief. Yet He still listens. And He still knows that I am here. My joy means as much to Him as my sorrow.

## Love Is Interested in Me

I am not a toy that God winds up and sends on its way. He knows everything that went into the creation of me, but He wants very much to find out what I am going to do with what I am. Seeing me and hearing me is not enough for Him. He wants to find out what is going on inside me, and that is something I can't always tell Him—because I don't always know. Or understand. So He makes His own inquiries into the state of my being

How?

By dropping His guard. By getting so close to me that He might get hurt when I strike out at Him in anger or frustration or foolishness. By remembering His own experience of what it is to be human so that He can understand what I can't put into words. By recalling the sting of tears, the downward pull of doubt, the queasiness of fright, the paralysis of worry, the hunching forward of want, the clench of having, the sudden reach of giving, and the slow hesitancy of taking back.

He sees what I might be, and He knows what I am. But He makes no comment on the distance between the two.

## Love Is Concerned about the Distance

How am I going to get from here to there? That is what bothers God. Oh, yes, He could move me from one space to another—if He had wanted me to be a chess piece. And I'm sure there are times when He wishes I were. But He gave me the right to determine where I am going. Which left Him with the right to worry about what is going to happen to me along the way.

I know that He is concerned. I would like to end His

anxiety, and I try to. Honestly. But, also honestly, I often think I know exactly what I am doing and I ignore His cautioning comments. At times, in fact, I wish He would stop worrying about me because I don't like knowing that I am making Him uncomfortable. I'm fine! Let me be!

Yet I'm not. And I soon find that out. But there He is, still worrying. And I am very glad that He is because I need His caring. It heals me. It strengthens my resolve to go out and try again. Yes, again I have His concern. I can count on it. It gives both of us a hard time. But it also gives a way of saying, however gruffly, "You matter to me."

## Love Appreciates Me

I used to think that appreciation meant someone liked what I did or said or was, and told me so.

My mistake.

When I say that God appreciates me, I mean that I am accurately perceived. I cannot impress God with what I am, nor can I discourage Him with what I am not.

I'm sure He has hopes that I will improve. But He also knows how difficult it is for me to grow. He's been here. He knows how insistently we are pulled and tugged to be what others want us to be. He knows the seductive power of our own dreams.

He doesn't add to the pressure. He never reminds me that I am not living up to my potential. He doesn't tell me how much more He has to do because I am not there to help. He never mentions what He has done for me.

If He is disappointed in me, He doesn't say so. Nor does He let me find out for myself. Because that isn't the way He feels. He doesn't dwell on what I haven't achieved. He concentrates, instead, on what I have been able to do in this world. It may not amount to much in my eyes, but He seems to think I have done well. He seems to think I will do better, but He isn't asking for promises. He doesn't ask me to please Him, but He does want me to learn who I am. I truly believe that no matter how well or how badly I turn out, it will not change the way God feels about me.

## Love Is Right Here

Some people call it commitment. I call it presence. We can commit from a distance, and while that may be noble, it isn't always love.

Love gets right next to you. It looks you straight in the eyes. It does more than hear what you say. It sees the expression on your face as you say the words. And you know that, should you need the presence of love, it will drop whatever it is doing and cross whatever distance there is between you to be at your side.

It asks nothing in the way of thanks for this inconvenience. Love is happy to be with you. It's on your side. It knows what you're trying to do with your life, and it wants you to succeed. You can lean on its shoulder now and then, but not too hard. It will help you to stand but it won't carry you where you can very well walk by yourself. It will turn a deaf ear if you talk about giving up. It may shake you roughly if you say the word *can't*. But if you *really* can't, love will hold you close for as long as it takes you to realize that you don't have to prove anything. You're lovable. The way you are. And, frankly, having love this close to you makes you realize you must be worth something.

## Love Speaks My Language

I pray. And it helps me to know that I can actually talk to God. I listen while I pray, and often I can sense God talking to me. But there are times when I can't find the words to describe what I mean. Or what I feel. Or don't feel. And there are times when I think God is talking to me, but I can't hear a word He says.

Love looks for alternate ways to communicate, and if I can't get through to God, He always finds a way to get through to me. He uses some incredibly innovative channels, but I have learned never to question them. The aging robin, for instance, who sounded a sweet racket outside my back door for the longest time before it occurred to me that he was trying to get my attention. And then when I saw him, more gray-breasted than red, and keeping to the low branches because he couldn't fly very high, I wondered where he got the strength to chirp at all. He seemed very old. He didn't move away when I stepped outside, and then I saw an enormous worm lying on the path, too still to be alive. But every time the robin moved toward it, younger birds came out of the trees and fought him off. So I walked over to the worm and stood there until the robin made a meal of it. Then I crumbled some bread and placed it in low protected spaces under shrubs where they could be reached and eaten safely. The next day the crumbs were gone, and my stalwart old friend was back chirping for more. I fed him for several days, during which time he seemed to grow robust. Then I never saw him again.

So—I helped a bird. Where does God's love fit into that?

I felt useful, and at that particular time in my life it was something I needed badly. I'm a person who likes to get things done, and I find it almost unbearable to believe that there is no solution to a problem. Surely, *something* can be done! Well, I was learning that it isn't always so. I hadn't been able to do anything to help a close family member who was seriously ill. Not even her doctors were hopeful she would survive.

I had prayed. Then I couldn't pray anymore, at least not

in words. I couldn't get through to God, but He got through to me. He understood how agonizing helplessness can be, and He knew I needed to feel effective about something. Feeding the bird did it. Being able to *do* something—especially to prolong life—was the only language I could understand at that time. And love used it.

Being loved by God changes us. Not always in an obvious way. We may look the same, we may have the same quirks and mannerisms. We endear ourselves or become a nuisance for the same reasons we did before. What changes is our ability to do things we never were able to do. We make better use of what we are and what we have. To put it in a nutshell, we discover how to give ourselves—without losing ourselves.

Because they learned how it felt to be loved by God, a handful of men and women were able to teach the world what real love is. And at great risk. They didn't have to become heroic; they remained ordinary. Even the weakest among them didn't become stronger, or the cautious become bold or the petty become magnanimous. But they didn't have to pretend to be admirable in order to get love. They already *had* it. For nothing. And it was love itself that provided what they needed in order to do what they did.

Sitting on the stairs, rubbing my aching shin, on a gray summer afternoon, I knew I was not the same as I had been. I felt good about myself—for no reason. Then I thought about the three friends I had lost, and the way I felt about them was different, too. There was no anger, no blame or guilt. I didn't defend myself for my failures, nor did I excuse theirs. The artist used to exhaust my patience because she tried so hard to be perfect that she couldn't finish a project. The writer couldn't keep track of time and said yes to more work than he could handle. The other writer was so caught up in exciting ideas that he paid no attention to details. And I was always coming up with answers to their problems, and never understanding why they didn't like—or use —my solutions. I saw them as I was beginning to see myself, all of us trying so hard to win one another's admiration when we were already lovable.

Looking back over our broken relationship, I could even smile a little because I was beginning to love my lost friends. Not as I thought I had loved them—but as *I* was loved.

Was it easy?

No. But possible.

It occurs to me now that I'm not the easiest person in the world to love. If you want to spend time with me, you will have to put up with the company of my dog and cat, who are very dear to me. I will not close them up in another room, and although I insist on their observing a certain amount of good manners, you will have to encounter their affection. Or their disdain, which can be embarrassing to you. My dog will investigate your purse or your pocket and try to steal anything that interests her, so be careful where you put your possessions. My cat will not tolerate it if you want to read and will lie on your book, magazine, or newspaper until you acknowledge that he is far more interesting than anything in print.

Beyond my animals, there is also the way I like to live that might present problems to you. As much as I may enjoy your company, I absolutely require a certain amount of time to myself. I have a generous supply of energy, especially in the morning, when I can be annoyingly enthusiastic—about anything, including the fact that it's a new day. But I burn out early in the evening, and I need a lot of sleep so I can get up early, which I prefer. Late nights unsettle my routine for days, and I resent them.

I am deeply interested in you and in everything you are doing, but if I am thinking about an idea I'm developing for a book, I won't hear a word you say. I won't even hear a word *I* say to you—until I finish doing the work in my head. But I will sense how you are feeling. I will share your pain, perhaps more than you would like me to; and because I want so much to help you end your pain, I may give you more comfort than you want. I can be a pest. I will try to help you, but I have difficulty asking you to help me. So I will have to rely on you to understand that even though I don't always articulate my needs, I do have them. God has given me a fair amount of strength, but He has also given me sensitivity, so don't be fooled by my self-sufficiency. I want you near me. I want you in my life, and I want to be in yours. But as the person I am and the person you are. I don't want to become a myth again.

But—I can't speak for everyone.

We all know people, some of them close to us, who spend their lives searching for love when, to us at least, it seems they are surrounded by it. They aren't being difficult or greedy; they just can't recognize love when they see it because they want it to be something else. They want it to be admiration.

Christ had the same difficulty telling us He loved us. We didn't like the way He said it. We liked our words better. We said, "Do you love me?" But Christ said, "Will you allow Me to love you?" We said, "I love you because you're wonderful," and He said, "My loving you is wonderful."

## Not Everyone Wants to Be Loved

While it is true that wherever Christ went, He drew a crowd, many more people stayed away from Him. And even among those who went with Him, many turned back. I'm tempted to ask, "Why?" and yet I suspect that, had I been there, I, too, might have been one who said, "Thanks—but no."

Because, as wonderful as it is to be loved by God, that is not the end of the experience. The next step is to give what we have been given. And that is the hard part.

I would not have wanted to be with Him when they arrested Him. I would not have wanted to be so alone after all the friends, including me, ran off. I don't really know how I could have gone on loving them, but then I am not God. I would have insisted that I was, after all, only human. But He would not have accepted that from me. He would have reminded me that there was a lot of me in Him. He would have called my attention to His pain, which He felt as much as I would. He would have confessed to me that there were times when He didn't want to suffer on my account. That He even tried to get out of it. And He could have. Except that it would have meant that He stopped loving. And loving was an important part of who He was.

It is the most important part of who we are. It delivers us from myths, from the heartbreak of offering what we *are not* to someone who *is not*. It enables us to give instead our real selves, and in the giving to discover who we are.

But loving, like being loved, is something we have to learn. From God.

# 3

---

# To So Love

---

THERE IS a very good reason why Jesus Christ, just before He died, told us to love one another as He loves us. Having been among us, He saw what most of us have difficulty seeing: that we love each other badly.

We are clumsy, unintentionally unkind, and confused—because we have never learned how to love. Yet most of us would be surprised to discover that there is anything about love we don't already know. We prefer to think of love as a feeling—of mysterious origin and quite beyond our control. But it isn't. Love is a way of life—a good way, but not an easy one.

I used to wince whenever someone spoke of "working at" a relationship. To me, it meant that something wasn't real. Or spontaneous. Or maybe that something was over and it would be better if we all admitted it and got on with our lives. Marriage, for instance. If two people are in love, then why shouldn't their marriage be good? I thought that if a man and woman had to "work at" their marriage, then there probably wasn't any love left in it, and no amount of work was going to put it back.

I also thought that if parents had to "work at" being parents, then they really didn't love their children. Family life seemed as simple as that: You loved your kids, and they

43

loved you back. Or you didn't, and neither did they. Being a parent seemed to be a natural part of being human; if you didn't have the talent, you were in trouble, and so were your children.

I was drawing a line right down the middle: Love was a gift from God; working at it was a poor human imitation. People who loved each other didn't have problems. If you had problems, then you didn't have love. That was the way I looked at life and love and people when I was younger. Now I know a bit more about love—mostly that I was absolutely wrong about what it is and where it comes from.

Experts assure us that we do, indeed, have to work at love. It may begin spontaneously, but it certainly doesn't remain that way. Love grows stale, we are told, but there are countless things we can do to revive that early attraction. We must talk to each other, listen to each other, let each other know what we are feeling, even to the point of arguing fiercely when we don't agree. This, we are promised, will bring us closer to each other, and the closer we get, the better—and longer—we can love. We must allow each other to grow and change, hopefully at the same pace and in the same direction. But if we lose step with each other—no matter whether we are parent, child, or marriage partner—then we must part company. Because we owe a certain amount of love to ourselves, and we must not let anyone deprive us of it.

While all these bits of advice may be true and helpful, they only teach us how to behave. Not how to love. Nor do they tell us how long it will take us to grow into loving human beings. Nor what to do when we get close enough to see things in each other that we do not like and may not be able to improve. All the words in the world, and all the hours of attentive listening are not going to ease the disappointment we experience when the one we love doesn't seem lovable anymore. And if we do part company in order to salvage a few remnants of love for ourselves, we may find that our kind of love can't help us any more than it could help the others in our life. Our needs may have outgrown it.

For a large portion of my life I loved the way a child loves. I wanted my needs met; I needed care, protection, affection, an enormous amount of assurance that nothing terrible was going to happen to me in a world filled with terrible possibilities. I wasn't capable of giving love or meeting anyone else's needs—unless that person just happened to need a little girl who needed loving. The ability to give love has to come later in life—except that for most of us it doesn't. We resist it. We sense that it means we are going to get hurt, and, like children, we pull back from a painful experience. And so, as far as love is concerned, we remain children, keeping more and more distant from anything that might make us cry. At the same time we remain strangers to what is best in ourselves: the qualities that only loving can reveal and strengthen. In a sense, you could say that love is a part of us that God knows is there, and we don't.

Love doesn't grow spontaneously. It has to be learned, and the only qualified Teacher we have is God, who has already been where we have to go. And it will take us the rest of our lives to become educated. We may also change radically.

So—you can understand why real love, between people who know they are real, is never easy. We do have to work at it, but not in the sense that we have to alter the way we behave. The change has to go deeper than that. We have to become altered by loving.

## To Love and Not to Like

When I adopted my cat, Mr. Jones, he was a totally new experience for me. Until then I knew more about dogs. So Mr. Jones had to teach me what I needed to know about cats. And how to love one.

For the first five years of his life, Mr. Jones lived indoors. My house was on a busy street where too many cars passed by, and I couldn't endure the minute-by-minute possibility that my cat might be killed. Mr. Jones accepted his confinement until I moved to a quieter area where he could smell the country air. Naturally he wanted to get out into it. With some misgivings, I let him out, only during the day, but I watched him closely. He rubbed himself against various parts of the house, fixing his scent on it, going a little farther each day and then running back to the safety of indoors. Finally he knew his way around and would remain outside for hours at a time. But he always came when I called him. Feeling I had provided for his well-being, I breathed more easily.

Then one day I heard him at the door making a growling sound that was new to me. To my horror, I saw that he had brought home a baby rabbit, only half alive. He had caught it and was mauling it on the front steps. It was his gift to me. My only thought was to save the rabbit, but it was too late, and a compassionate neighbor put the animal out of its agony. But first I had to pull my cat away from his prey. Mr. Jones allowed me to do it because he trusted me not to hurt him. And as I picked him up, I felt myself literally being torn in two between my love for him and my revulsion at what he had done. I held him close to me until my neighbor removed the dead rabbit, and then I brought Mr. Jones into the house.

I kept him indoors the rest of the day but I couldn't go

near him. Puzzled by the absence of love, he stared at me with those pale jade eyes of his, but he made no attempt to approach me. Inside of me a war was going on. Could I go on loving this cat who could kill a helpless rabbit? What kind of person was I?

It took a few hours for me to find out. I also grew a little as love asked me some tough questions. Such as: Now that the cuddly part of loving my cat was over, how did I feel about a creature who had a streak of cruelty in him? Or was it cruelty? Wasn't my cat's primitive instinct a part of him? And didn't God provide him with that instinct as well as the remarkable agility that enabled him to climb trees and perform daring acrobatics on a narrow branch—all of which I found delightful? Could I insist that Mr. Jones be exactly as I wanted him to be at all times? And when he did something that to me was horrible, yet to him was perfectly natural, was it fair of me to make him feel despised? Could I split my love down the middle—loving what was huggable and entertaining about him and ignoring what was abhorrent?

Well, the answer was that none of these solutions spelled love, because love doesn't exclude anything. In my relationship with Mr. Jones, I was meeting the same dilemma God meets in loving me: I did not like everything about the creature I loved. And probably I never would. Love had to teach me how to accept what I couldn't abide.

If I love you, that doesn't mean I approve of everything you do. And I'll be honest about it. You'll know it when I don't like something. Maybe I won't be able to change it. Maybe it's something you think is perfectly all right and necessary, and I don't. But I won't pretend it isn't there. I'll see it, I'll call it by name, and I'll acknowledge the fact that you may disagree with me.

I'll accept you the way God accepts me. I'll take into my

environment of care what I find abhorrent in you. I'll be concerned about its effect on your life. I'll share whatever pain it causes you. I will fight it—but I will not fight you. I will not allow what I do not like in you to come between you and my loving you—anymore than God allows my sin to keep Him from loving me. Loving you will teach me how to distinguish between you and what you do.

## Love Is a Caretaker

Because I love my cat, it isn't enough for me to look out for his well-being. I have to look out for the well-being of those he may harm. I have to be responsible for my loved one's liabilities because, when I accepted them, I made them my concern.

To me, a baby rabbit or a young bird used to be something sweet to sigh over. Not anymore. I know them now as helpless creatures, utterly unable to defend themselves against the aggressiveness of an animal I love. I cannot ignore their plight. While I cannot guarantee safety for all of them, I can make a difference to a few.

Loving a predator has made me more observant. I watch what happens when Mr. Jones disappears into the bushes. Bluejays screech and hover. Smaller birds take flight. Rabbits, however, go on eating grass, not at all wary because squirrels are dashing past them for cover. Because I can tell when Mr. Jones is in a hunting mood, very often I can warn off his intended victims. I slam a door or open a window noisily. Sometimes I take a casual walk in the endangered area. Love has made me a caretaker. It has also taken my caring far beyond my cat and our immediate surroundings. It has made me my brother's keeper—and the keeper of those my brother cannot keep.

Love, first of all, has awakened me to the realization that we human beings are not evenly divided between those who can look after themselves and those who cannot. At least, not all of the time. The most self-reliant among us come upon times of helplessness. And those who feel they have no authority quite suddenly may find that they do.

But there are those among us whose situations do not fluctuate as much as others'. Some of us come into this world with certain advantages of power, wealth, enlightenment, determination. We have the upper hand over those who are born to poverty, dependence, ignorance, and hopelessness. We are not quite the same as my cat and the young rabbits, predator and prey. But we aren't monsters and victims, either. We are lovable people doing harm to other lovable people, and much of the time we may look upon what we do as quite natural. We are a unique blend of weaknesses and strengths. And life is a tangle of opportunities and denials. In the melee of what we are and what we attempt, some of us wound others. And some of us, if wounded, cannot—because we are handicapped by our lack of advantages—defend ourselves.

Where does love fit into this picture? Not naturally. And not without effort.

Love brings the extremes together. It joins advantaged with deprived. It impels the strong to support the weak. It is the reason why the meek shall inherit the earth—because the meek is not one person, or many, but the one who is strong helping the one who is not. And there is nothing more durable. Only the two of us, joining hands, can attain what God so cherishes: meekness—which is, if anything, the strong yielding to those who are less strong. It is God yielding to us. And only love can make it happen.

No matter if I am not the one who caused you pain. Someone I love, somewhere, is causing another's pain, and my love makes me responsible. I cause pain, too, and there are those who love me. So let us heal one another, in the

name of love, even if we do not know one another. We
sense the need of comfort—and that is enough for love to
know.

## Love Isn't Always Satisfied

We cannot expect the person we love to give us everything we need. Yet we keep hoping.

I have already mentioned the writer who couldn't keep
track of time. But there was more to the man than that. If
ever a human being embodied kindness and good intentions, he did. He was always trying to solve problems—his
children's, his children's spouses' and their friends', his
wife's, his wife's mother's, yours, mine, anybody's. One
day he looked out his office window and saw an elderly
man trip and fall as he was crossing a busy street, so my
friend ran down four flights of stairs to offer his help. He
found ways to spend a lot of time with his wife, especially
when she was on chemotherapy following a mastectomy. If
you needed a wing to climb under, he had a big one, but
you would find it a very crowded place.

He wasn't efficient. He made promises he couldn't keep
and he let people down. He lost names and addresses as
soon as you gave them to him and he couldn't remember
appointments. He was so certain he would be rich and successful someday that he spent every dollar before he earned
it. And although he was an excellent writer, you knew he
would always be late with his manuscript.

Now—how do you love such a person? That was a question I had to ask myself because I did not want this man
and his kindness and his family to go out of my life. But
how was I going to put up with the impossible part of him?

By learning—from love, of all things—how to be independent.

I'm serious. And I make that statement because anyone who knows me knows that I always considered myself independent. I stood on my own two feet, thank you. I earned my own living, paid my own bills, suffered for my own mistakes, made my own decisions, and asked no favors. Or so I liked to think about myself.

The truth is, I was quite dependent—on those I loved. Because I wanted them to give me what I should have given myself.

If I loved you, then I expected you to enrich every part of my life. If I thought you were very wise, I would pay close attention to your advice and follow it to the letter—even if it went against my own judgment. If I liked the way you dressed, I would let you tell me how to dress, even if I was uncomfortable wearing what you chose. If you were a superb tennis player, I would assume you also were a superb swimmer, golfer, runner, or anything else athletic. If you liked the theater as much as I did, then I was certain you would enjoy everything else I enjoyed. I would, by loving you, make you responsible for my well-being. And I would be terribly disappointed if you satisfied only some of my needs, not all.

Because my writer friend was a good writer, I assumed he also had a good head for business, and I jumped at the chance to work with him. It was a mistake—mine, not his.

Had I been as independent as I thought I was, I could have loved my friend for his goodness and asked no more of him. By expecting him to be as good a worker as he was a friend, I was asking him to make our business relationship as successful as our friendship was. And that's not an independent way to live. My work—and the success of it—is my responsibility, not anyone else's.

I couldn't ignore my friend's irritating work habits, but I

could certainly accept them as long as I didn't depend on them. If my car broke down late at night a million miles from nowhere, and if I could get to a phone, I could call my friend, wake him out of a sound sleep, and he would come to wherever I was and see me safely home. No big deal—I needed help, and he could help me. No dependence, either. I was looking out for myself, going to the person who was best able to give me what I needed in a specific situation.

But—asking my friend to look over a contract and then agonizing because he couldn't remember where he put it was neither sensible nor fair nor looking out for myself. It was asking my friend for something he didn't have, and then blaming him for depriving me of it. It was avoiding my responsibility to work with someone who could give me what I needed in that part of my life: efficiency.

Independence, I discovered, is not a matter of making up my mind. It is obtaining the information I need to make an objective decision. It is going to the person who can give me what I need. And that isn't always someone I love.

But—how was I to restore the broken friendship? By doing exactly what God often does for me: by letting my love speak in a language my friend could hear. Going over what happened would have been useless; we never had been able to communicate about it. I couldn't say, "I'm sorry," and neither could he; each of us thought the other was to blame. But my friend is a man who likes to be with people, and he also likes to eat. So I invited him and his wife and a few mutual friends to dinner. I was trying to say, "I love you," and the message got through. We spent a lovely evening without even mentioning our disastrous business venture. We both knew what had happened and we had gained something from it: an appreciation of our friendship and a determination never to ask more of each other than we could give. The friendship, incidentally, has lasted.

## Some Things You Have to Do Alone

I used to wonder how Christ could go on loving us after that night in Gethsemane. After He asked for so little, and we couldn't give it to Him. *Come and sit up with me*, He asked of us. And we couldn't stay awake. *I'm going to die, and I don't want to wait alone*, He explained. And we nodded drowsily—*of course, we would, what are friends for?*—and fell asleep again.

We have all known such times. Not only in the face of death, but in the face of fear or dread or loss or a terrible uncertainty. We feel isolated, unprotected on all sides, infinitesimally small and weak in the shadow of something terrifyingly vast. It is not a good time to be alone. If ever we need someone close to us, someone to stand by our side, this is it. If anyone loves us, now is the time to prove it. *Be with us!*

And when there is no reply, or at best a yes, yes, I'll be there in a moment—but the moment never comes—we know that we cannot possibly go on loving someone who can let us down so cruelly.

Or can we?

Christ could.

But He was of God.

He was of us, too. Especially in that dark night of need, He was excruciatingly human. He had doubts about Himself, just as we do. He wasn't sure He wanted to keep His promise to us, and we all know how that feels. He didn't want to die, He didn't want to leave, He didn't want to suffer, and neither do we. But He didn't want to let God down, either. He just wanted someone to understand how

He felt, what He was going through. He wanted someone to realize what He was trying to do. Don't we all? And aren't we, like Christ, asking too much of someone we love?

There are some things we cannot share with anyone—except God. There are times when no one—except God—can go through our experience with us. Because no one, at least no human being, can become so much a part of us that he or she feels our pulsebeat, inhales our breath, perceives what we see, hear, smell, and touch, or feels the words catch in our throat. We can only imagine such moments in the life of another, but we cannot *become* that person. Only God can. Between ourselves and any other person, no matter how precious we are to each other, there is always a thin curtain of individuality that keeps us apart, that allows us to feel the anxious push of the fingers against the push of ours, but we cannot feel flesh against flesh. There is that gauzy veil in the way.

But not in the way of God—because He does not have to come to us. He is already here, a part of us. He is more than our Creator. He feels, senses, knows what we do just as keenly as if He were us—which He is.

If you cannot come to me in my time of need, yes, I can still love you. Because I may have asked you to come too far. I may have asked you to live for me, and you can't do that. You can only live *with* me.

## How Can I Get to Where You Are?

Suppose, though, that you and I are separated by more than a gauzy veil? Suppose I have put some distance between us because I don't like what I saw up close?

You may want more than I want to give you. You may not give me enough. Perhaps you lied to me. Took something from me. Hurt me. How am I to go on loving you? How can I close the distance between us when I don't even want to take a step in your direction?

I'm forgetting something.

I've been thinking of my own needs. And of yours, too. I've been concerned with how much I can give to you and still have enough for myself. I'm forgetting that my greatest need—and yours, too—is to love. If I cannot love, then I am denying myself access to what is best in me. I am making it harder for God to go on creating me through the productive use of me. You are doing the same to yourself. We may like to think that we don't need each other, but the truth is that we do need to love each other. Just as God needs to love us in order to be God. Just as we never would have learned who or what He is if He hadn't come to us across the distance that used to separate us. He called it forgiveness, this coming to where we are. We may call it reconciliation—same thing. Whichever word we use, we have to learn how to live it because it's a form of love that isn't natural to us. It is to God.

Forgiveness is not a ritual. It is not a forced smile from a cold heart. It is my walking barefoot over rough ground to get to you because you cannot—or will not—come to me, and the pain is intense. There is no cause to smile, and my heart is hot with anger over what you have done to my love. Forgiveness is my loving you in the hardest way possible, and I can't do it alone. You can't help me, I know that. But God can, because this is His kind of love, not ours.

Recently a friend and I were talking about a news story we found hard to believe. It concerned a young man who murdered his mother, went to prison for it, and during the many years he was there his relationship with God began.

He felt loved, forgiven. He experienced such a deep spiritual friendship with Jesus Christ that he wanted to share it with others who thought no one could possibly love them. After serving his sentence, he became a minister, and now he has been accepted as an assistant pastor in a church whose congregation knows the facts about his crime and punishment.

My first reaction was that the congregation was well intentioned but unrealistic. "I hate to say this," I said out loud, "but he'll never work out." And even as I spoke those words, I realized I was wrong.

The congregation was more than well intentioned. They were trying to do what they knew was right, what Christ Himself did for us. And it wasn't natural to them. They were trying to experience *true* forgiveness, and that is divine—because in order to achieve it we have to reach beyond our human ability to love. In fact, we have to love so hard that we break through to the God-part of ourselves.

If you do something to hurt me, then I won't want to get close to you for fear of being hurt again. You may, from your distance, hold your arms out to me, and tears may run down your face; you may be telling me that you are aware of the harm you have done and you may insist that you want never to do such harm again. Nevertheless, I don't want to go to you alone. In all honesty, I can't. I'm not that brave. God will have to go with me. Because you are not the only one I fear. I'm afraid of myself. In my anger at what you have done to my love, I want to retaliate. At the very least I want to see you grovel and submit to some form of punishment.

But on my way to where you are, something happens. Each step costs me pain, and I feel it sharply. But the pain doesn't last. It is healed, and something else takes its place. I feel God's love for me, and it so encompasses me that I am transformed by it. My anger, my desire to strike you down, and my will to see you suffer are accepted—with distaste—and I am embraced.

I'm not afraid anymore. I want to embrace you, even though you may hurt me again. I know now that I can turn my other cheek because I am strong enough to survive the blow, not because it will not hurt. I won't excuse the blow; I'll call it what it is: an injury. My love will take as many blows as you may give, but it will never call them by any other name. My love will suffer pain, but will never agree that it is justified. I will not encourage the evil that is in us all by calling it good. I will not accept your insistence that what you did was somehow for my own benefit—I will not let you, Judas-like, destroy me with a kiss. I am made knowledgeable by love. I can risk getting close to you without closing my eyes to what I see.

Don't look away. Don't brace yourself for my denunciation. There won't be any.

My hand goes out to you. Not in anger, but to lift you up so that you and I can look into each other's eyes. So that you and I can see God there—and know who made such loving possible.

## What If . . . ?

Ideally, you and I should remain as close as we are now. But that doesn't always happen. You may not even respond to my outstretched hand, and although I have come to where you are, you may draw back from me. What have I gained from all my loving?

A lot.

I know now what it is to be a loving person. I don't want to be any other kind, and that will influence the way I live.

For instance . . .

Normally I am fairly patient. But a young man named

Paul was taking too much of my time and seemed unaware that I had other things to do. Paul wrote poetry; he called himself a poet, but I didn't because he wasn't published and I'm a bit of a snob about such things. He was referred to me by a friend who thought I might help him in his work and who didn't listen when I said I really didn't know much about poetry. Paul didn't listen, either, when I said I was busy.

Would I read a poem? he asked.

I couldn't bring myself to say no.

Would I read a few?

All right.

His poems were excellent. I didn't have to be an expert to realize that. He had a fine creative talent, and I told him so. It was my undoing.

Paul got to me by telephone, by letters and notes, and sometimes by ringing my doorbell and handing me his latest revisions as he backed off, apologizing for interrupting my work.

Finally, to Paul's great pleasure and mine, a small literary magazine published two of his poems. I thought that would end, or at least cut down, his intrusion into my life. But, no, he wanted to thank me for my encouragement, and he couldn't stop. The calls, the letters, the sound of the doorbell went on. I knew I had to find a way to discourage him, but it was difficult because Paul didn't stay long enough for me to explain what a nuisance he was.

Then he called to tell me that his mother wanted me to come to dinner. Would I?

I lied.

I didn't call it that—I called it "finding a way out." I said I had other plans for that day. Sorry. Thank you.

I had taken the first step. The others would be easier. Let the phone ring, don't answer the doorbell, throw the letters out unopened. Cut off communication. I had done enough. Too much. I needed time to work. I needed to love. And I was miserable without it. I did not like *not* being a loving person.

The phone rang a few times, unanswered. Paul sent a note or two, telling me that another magazine was interested in his poems. But the endless intrusions diminished. I was left to myself, to this person who didn't seem to be me.

I had put some distance between what I am naturally and what God knows I can be. So the two of us, God and I, had to make the journey to where I was. I suppose you could say I had to forgive myself. And when I did, I went straight to the phone and called Paul.

He was alarmingly respectful. I say *alarmingly* because I didn't deserve his respect. I had lied to him, and I was uncomfortable because he still looked up to me—only more so. He was a poet now, a professional even to my way of thinking, and he was learning the value of time. He knew that he had taken a lot of my time and he was apologetic.

But I was learning something, too. I was fortunate to have something, such as time, to give to another human being. Actually very little had been asked of me, and as grudgingly as I gave my love, I had gained from it.

"Paul," I said, "why don't you ask your mother to invite me to dinner again? I'd really love to come."

"You would?" he said. "You *really* would?"

"More than anything I can imagine," I said. I was beginning to feel at home with myself again, and it was good.

Being a loving person—now that I knew what such a person was—would cost me time, at least where Paul was concerned. Loving others would cost me in other ways. Energy. Thought. Consideration. Understanding. Patience. Interest. Respect. Care. Responsibility.

It gets harder. Loving will cost me disappointment, inconvenience, disagreement, anger, insult, injury. But never honesty. Never self-respect. Those I will get from loving. From walking from where I am to where you are—not by myself, but in the company of God.

Love is not a good compromiser. If God had met us half-way, there would still be a vast amount of distance between Him and us. Because we never could have made it halfway to Him; we were too weakened by our loss of love. He had to make up the difference. But He was weary, too, and for a long time we shouted at each other across the distance, God telling us what was wrong with us and our telling Him we were doing the best we could. Nothing we said to each other brought us any closer. And so, finally, because we needed to be loved and He needed to love, God closed the distance between us by throwing His own Self into the breach. He so loved that He gave us Himself and asked nothing in return. That's what reconciliation is—a giving of the part of ourselves that love has enabled us to discover. And yet we don't lose what we give; it brings us to the one we love and forms a bond between us that nothing can break. It's like the cross—it happened, and nothing can alter that fact.

*We love*—even if we are not loved back. We have reached the point of no return.

# 4

## Love Is Hard to Get Along With

I AM ABOUT TO LOSE a friend I value very much. And it's love that is straining the friendship.

Because I care about my friend, I feel it when she gets hurt. Unfortunately she gets hurt a lot because she doesn't place enough value on herself. She allows people to use her. She accepts blame for other people's errors. She is talented, hardworking, underpaid, and underappreciated. And if none of these facts were important to her, then I wouldn't be concerned. But they are important. I have listened to her anguish and disappointment when someone lets her down—again. I have wept with her. And I have seen her put on a placid smile in front of others and tell them that, no, she didn't mind, she didn't even notice, please don't worry, she's just fine.

Well, *I'm* not fine, and I have been telling my friend how it feels to see her make the same mistakes over and over again. I have tried to make it clear that I love her no matter how many mistakes she makes, and that I am speaking out of my own pain at seeing her hurt. But she hears only my anger. She sees only my disagreement. We are not getting along as well as we did, and because we aren't, my friend doesn't think we can possibly continue as friends.

She couldn't be more wrong. Love and getting along are not the same thing.

There is a distance between us all, and we want it that way. None of us wants to be known. And if one of us comes too close to the other and sees what we ourselves don't want to make known, we turn away from such scrutiny. We want nothing to do with that kind of love.

But—there isn't any other kind of love.

Love is not a feeling, warm and tingling. It is not "something" that comes over us, much like a mood and lasting about as long. *Love is us.* Close in. Revealed and revealing. Nothing more. And absolutely nothing less.

## The War between Our Genuine Selves

If you and I love each other, we will not always get along. We will not always speak politely out of our fear of offending—because we won't have such fear. We will not feel compelled to approve of each other. We will admire some qualities in each other, but certainly not all. We will not try to confirm what we know isn't true: such as that we are perfect. We will point a finger at the imperfections in each other, and that will not be comfortable. At times we will defend our myths and we will hurt each other in that defense. We will have to strike hard to tear down each other's excuses. And even if we hoist each other up on our respective shoulders after the conflict, we will nevertheless bear the bruises we inflicted on each other. But all this is love.

Love has atrocious manners. It will not tell us what we want to hear. It will tell us what is true and right and good. And we will reply that such things are poppycock, that the world doesn't live that way and never did. But love will not give ground; it will stick to what it knows is real. It will insist on knowing all there is to know about itself and the one who is loved. As you can imagine, love has to get very close to do that.

If you and I love each other, then we are not going to stand by quietly and watch us do harm to ourselves. If you are your own worst enemy, if you will do anything to gain the world's acceptance, then I am going to protest—because I cherish what is genuine in you and don't want to see it put aside. You may not listen to my protests. You may even resent them and accuse me of trying to run your life—and that will hurt me terribly. You may go on about your business and damage your life in the process. But you will not change the way I feel about you. You may put distance between you and me once again, but it will not be the same as it was. Because I have broken through to you and I know well the route.

If you and I love each other—in the way Christ loves us—it will not be because we are perfect. Far from it. If we come close enough to love, then we will know what there is in each of us that is good and admirable and decent—but also what is not. And we will not make excuses for what is not. In fact, because we love each other, we will throw our weight on the side of what is good and hope our love will make the difference in the struggle going on within each of us. We may grieve when what is good in the one we love is overwhelmed by what is not, but we will never pretend that it didn't happen. Nor will we stop loving each other—because we know the person we love, and we know what a risk we take to love at all.

## Don't Be Nice—Be You

This is a tale of two families.

One is more familiar to most of us. They got along so

well, the parents hardly ever raising their voices to each other, the children well behaved as far as anyone could tell. Their roles were clearly specified: The wife brought up the children and took care of the house, the husband worked and made their life-style possible, the children went to school. The grandparents—well, they came to dinner on the first Sunday of the month and seemed to be enjoying life.

Then everything was different.

The wife went back to school and soon she got a job. The husband came home later and later and finally stayed away for days at a time. The children's grades began to slide, and there were rumors of a brush with the police. The grandparents—nobody knew what happened to them because they stopped coming to dinner.

Before long there was no place where anyone could come to dinner. The house was sold, the divorce was granted, the wife and children squeezed themselves into a tiny apartment, the husband was said to be living with a younger woman. And the grandparents? As I said, nobody knew what happened to them, but everybody supposed that they probably were all right because when you're that old, your problems are behind you.

Nevertheless a shiver went through the neighborhood where the family had lived. It wasn't the first time a family had broken apart. In fact, it was becoming unusual for a family to stay together. And those who were still together began to wonder—Would it happen to them? But, no, they told themselves, they got along so well.

And now for the other family.

It was very noisy in that house because when anyone had something to say, out it came. I guess you wouldn't call it arguing, but they certainly had some heated discussions. They were so different from one another that it was hard to figure out how they got along at all.

The wife, for instance. She had something to do with stocks. Went to work every day, and on weekends she holed up in a little office in the basement, writing articles for a business magazine. The husband was in real estate and worked odd hours. The children had to help out with meals and cleaning the house, which wasn't always neat. But the kids had a lot of friends, and most of the time their friends came to their house. They seemed to like it there. Even when the eighty-six-year-old grandfather was visiting, which was quite often. He could tell some great stories, or so the young people said.

It wasn't unusual to see one of the kids, or even one of the parents, come slamming out the front door, mad as could be. But they'd always be back together again at night as if nothing had happened. If they left the curtains open, you could see them all laughing about something that happened. Or, every now and then, continuing one of those heated discussions.

The house is a little quieter now because the children have gone off in all directions. One's a math teacher, one's trying to get his songs published, and the youngest, the girl, is studying forestry. The grandfather? He still comes to dinner. And he still tells those great stories.

When the whole family gets together for the holidays, they're just as noisy as always. And just as different. It's funny, but for people who don't get along very well, they seem to love one another a lot.

Love is good, but it isn't always nice. Christ wasn't always nice, but there is no disputing His goodness. Nice puts up with, never raises its voice, keeps the peace at all costs, never gets wrinkled, and doesn't sweat. Good is a boatrocker; it promises itself that it will pass by the money-changers without saying a word and ends up turning over their tables. Good breathes hard, sweats heavily, and wipes a grimy hand across its face in embarrassment at its bad manners. It would like to observe the amenities, but it can't always.

Nice accepts what we say we are. Good perceives the God-created person in each of us. Nice isn't always there when you need help; help can get messy. Good's always there, sleeves rolled up. But nice gets the seat of honor, while good often eats in the kitchen.

So—don't be fooled by appearances. Nice claims to be loving. Good is.

## Love Makes Demands

When I met a young woman I hadn't seen since she was a child, we had a lot of news to catch up on.

"What are you doing now?" I asked.

"I'm a teacher," she said.

"Which grade?"

She smiled in an odd way, as if she were searching for the right words. "It's not a grade—exactly," she said. "It's a special section. I teach the bad kids."

She gave me no time to react. "They're *not* bad," she said, as if I had called them that—and apparently some people did. "They're good kids," she went on. "But they do some things that aren't so good."

I was fascinated—first, by the fact that there was such a section in schools these days; and second, by the maturity in such a young teacher.

"Sounds like hard work," I said.

"It is, sometimes," she admitted.

"How do you get your point across?" I asked.

"I try to let them know that I love them," she said. "But I let them know when I don't love some of the things they do."

She was that rare kind of a teacher most of us have had at some point in life, even if we didn't qualify for a special section. Not a favorite teacher, by any means. The kind the other kids said was tough, the kind you dreaded.

I had a teacher like that in my senior year of high school. She taught English and she was thoroughly disgusted with our casual understanding of the subject. She was a tiny, sparrowlike woman with jet-dark eyes and thin, fragile fingers that somehow smashed chalk to bits against the blackboards. And she drilled us mercilessly on nightmarish subjects such as grammar, sentence structure, syntax, and—embarrassingly—spelling. "You will not graduate illiterate," she would vow as she assigned us homework. She was deaf to our groans.

I thought she gave me a hard time, and none of my other teachers did. I was a conscientious student, but as diligently as I tried to get a good grade from her—and I often succeeded—she always added a minus after it. I started calling her "No-Plus," and the name caught on.

My grades were important to me, not only for personal reasons, but because I was applying to colleges. And hoping to get some financial aid through a scholarship, which, in those days, wasn't easy to obtain. I was determined not to allow No-Plus to spoil my record, but she was impossible to please.

In the spring of that year, I had an attack of appendicitis, meaning that, between surgery and recuperation, I would miss a few weeks of school. It wasn't the loss of my appendix that bothered me; it was the time away from classes. How would I catch up? How would my grades be affected?

A few days after I came home from the hospital, a sparrowlike woman rang our doorbell, introduced herself to my mother, and asked if she could spend some time with me. Yes, it was No-Plus. She was the only one of my teachers who realized how important it was for me to keep my grades up—it seems she made it her business to know a lot about all her students. She wanted to help me keep up with my classwork, not only in her course, but in all my courses, and she had collected schedules and homework assignments from my other teachers. If I was willing, she said, she would stop by every afternoon after school and go over my work with me.

Naturally I agreed—although the prospect of working with No-Plus every day was less than pleasant. She was no different in my home than she was in her classroom: tough, demanding, stingy with praise. But some of her driving energy rubbed off on me. I began to ask more of myself and found that I had more to give. Learning, I discovered, was not a grueling process of memorizing dates and keeping the sequence of events straight; it was, and is, an exploration into life itself. It is a search for the future through an understanding of the past. It is a somewhat lopsided appreciation of our human ability to make progress even while taking two steps forward and one step back.

I began to enjoy school. I had never disliked it, but it had been something I had to get through. It changed. School became a place where I felt I belonged. School and I had something to give each other.

I did not, however, begin to enjoy No-Plus. I was properly grateful to her, and I said all the right words. But I was glad to get back to my warmer teachers. My grades were better than ever (I got an A minus from No-Plus), I was accepted by the college I hardly dared hope would take me, and I was awarded a small but crucial scholarship. In my first year of college I was also excused from Freshman English and allowed to take a much more interesting writing course because, as my advisor said with an admiring shake of her head, I had an unusually high degree of proficiency in English. I did tell that to No-Plus; I wrote her a note, and I'm sure a smile might have tugged at the corners of her tightly pressed lips.

I know now that No-Plus loved me. She loved all her students. And I can't say as much for many of the teachers I preferred to her. I think they did their best to make their classes fun, because perhaps they thought it would help us to learn. Yet I remember almost everything I learned from No-Plus—and hardly anything my more enjoyable, less loving teachers tried to teach me. The most important thing No-Plus taught me was to push myself to discover my limits—and I still try to meet her demands. Some of the energy she put into my well-being is a part of me I will never lose. I'm only sorry that I never got to tell her—but then it took me a long time to realize how love works.

Besides, since No-Plus was so skilled at loving, I don't think she expected anything in return. What she wanted— and didn't *always* get—was for her students to take what she had to give, and use it to find themselves.

## What We See Is What We Love

Don't get the idea that love goes around picking on people and telling them what's wrong with them.

If I love you, it isn't my responsibility to right what is wrong with you. Loving you doesn't mean I can make you over into my ideal person. I don't have that authority. You are already created, and my job is to help you grow into yourself. If there is something about you I don't like, it's irrelevant. I'll have to try to live with it. If there is something that gets in the way of your self-fulfillment, then that is where my opposition belongs. Even if I have to oppose you along the way.

But—how can I tell the difference between something that gets in *my* way and something that gets in *yours?*

By seeing you through the eyes of God rather than my own. By focusing on what is important to your becoming a whole person—instead of what is important to me. By putting up, as Christ did, with the braggishness of a Peter because underneath it all was the strength of a mountain in the making. Yet by staying Peter's murderous sword, even though he wielded it in Christ's defense, because Peter's value was in the expanding of life, not in the ending of it. By patiently allowing a Thomas to satisfy his irritating doubts because they were the only obstacles to an incredible human commitment. By accepting the nervous secrecy of a Nicodemus visit because the man had the courage to pursue truth. Yet by holding up a hand to the young man whose addiction to wealth would assassinate his more compassionate intentions.

Your need is to fulfill the self God made it possible for you to be. My need is to help you.

## A Risk Worth Taking

Left to our own devices, we would no doubt take our love where it is easy to find. Fortunately for us, God manages to uncover our best talents. He finds reasons to draw us into love, whether we like it or not.

Some years ago I was quite proud to be entrusted with the formation of an editorial department for a publisher who had very little money to spend on personnel. I advertised for proofreaders and copy editors in the usual way and received some impressive résumés—which I knew we couldn't afford. Nevertheless I conducted some interviews of men and women I wished I could hire, but when it came down to salary, the interview was over. Both my pride and my enthusiasm diminished rapidly. What was I to do?

It occurred to me—and I think God had something to do with putting the idea into my head—that there was a lot of talent "out there" among women who had brought up their children and were looking for something else to do. They had an education, ambition, and no experience. Okay. They would not expect much in the way of salary— maybe.

I ran an ad in the classified sections of local newspapers—under no particular heading, but aimed at attracting the very women I needed—women with ability and no place to use it, women more eager for the opportunity to learn than to make money. Opportunity was all I had to offer.

The responses were few. But valuable. The interviews left me humbled: These were women of character and amazing capacity. The question became: Could I give them what they needed to become first-class workers?

It was a trade-off—as love often is.

I had to make time to give them everything I knew (which was everything someone else had given to me) about reading galleys and editing manuscripts so that they could use that expertise to sharpen their own talents. In the process I had to learn how to distinguish between what got in my way and what kept them from functioning.

When I hired three women whose children were grown and whose skills were rusty, I already liked them. I admired their courage to enter a world where younger people seemed to know what they were doing, even if they really didn't. So we were off to a harmonious start. But whenever people work or live together, the rough edges soon make their appearance, and we were no exception. One woman simply had to interrupt whatever I was doing to tell me about something ridiculous she had found in a manuscript. Another was so fastidious about checking dates and figures (which I hated) that I felt I could no longer trust the fact of my own birthday. Another talked incessantly, about anything.

For a time I thought my trade-off wasn't going to work. I was giving help instead of getting it.

The woman who talked a lot was the one who taught me something—with only a few words.

My dog died. She had been an unidentifiable mixture of several kinds of dogs, and I loved her dearly for twelve years. She had never been well and finally she had to give up trying to keep up with our family. Her name was Boots—because she was shiny black all over except for her white paws. I had very little experience with losing someone I loved, and my grief was sudden and devastating. For two days I couldn't go to work because I kept crying uncontrollably, and that was not appropriate conduct for an office environment.

When I returned to my desk, I found a letter there—from the talker. In a few lines she told me that she knew how I felt because she had lost a dog who was dear to her. That's all. Just signed: Catherine.

I knew then that Christ would have seen through Catherine much more quickly than I did. He would have seen that her incessant jabbering meant something that a psychologist might explain, and possibly could reduce—but it meant nothing to a loving relationship. It was not even something I could try to reduce, because it simply was in my way and not in hers.

What was in her way was the fact that she was a chain smoker, and it was killing her. Her conversation was frequently cut off by the most bone-chilling cough I have ever heard, yet she would wave her hand to signal that she didn't need help, even though she was gasping for breath. And the moment she could straighten up, she would reach for a cigarette.

I used to put up with Catherine's smoking just as I put up with her talking. Whenever she left my office, I would open the window and stand in front of it, breathing deeply, even in the middle of winter. Well, that helped me, but it didn't do anything for Catherine, and once I knew that I loved the woman, I had to do more.

Poor Catherine, I'm sure she didn't know what to make of my changed behavior, because I suddenly became a nag. I stopped whatever I was doing every time she lit a cigarette and told her she was killing herself. I frowned in disgust when she exhaled and waved the smoke out of my way. I made Catherine's habit extremely unpleasant for her and I wish I could say she gave it up. But, no, she had been attacked by better naggers than I was, and she refused to give in. Obviously the problem went deeper than the desire to smoke, and I never found out what it was. Perhaps I would have, except that I gave up my crusade when it became evident that it was coming between Catherine and me, and I didn't want to lose her friendship. I felt guilty, too, about making her life so miserable. I had not learned the art of loving to the point where I could make it clear to Catherine that I loved her but didn't love some of the things she did. I had to make that distinction in my own mind first, and I hadn't done that. I was still confusing loving with being nice.

Eventually Catherine and I went our separate ways for other reasons. Her husband retired, and they moved away, and I went out on my own. Every year since then, hers was the first Christmas card I received, and it always arrived two days after Thanksgiving. In her tiny script she could fill a card with a year's worth of news, and always ended with a nostalgic flashback to something that happened when we worked together. She thanked me far too much for giving her an opportunity to do some excellent work and never accepted the credit I tried to push on her.

And then the cards were written by someone else. The language was Catherine's but not the script, and the news was short and grim. Catherine was dictating to a nurse because she couldn't write anymore. She had advanced emphysema. She also had Alzheimer's disease and hoped I would excuse the fact that she rambled here and there. Sometimes she began a letter and then went into a forgetful phase and couldn't continue her thought for a few days.

Last year's card came very late, not until after New Year's Day. There were only a few words on it, and I thought I could see her struggling to remember who I was. Yet she sent her love to me and, again, thanked me too much.

For what? I thought. I hadn't loved her hard enough to risk our friendship. I should have snatched the cigarettes from her hand as she took them out of her purse. I should have smashed them right in front of her eyes or thrown them out the window or crushed them with my foot—or any of the ridiculously excessive things we sometimes do when we really love someone.

My greatest mistake was that I didn't offer Catherine what I asked of her. I gave her only my strengths and not my weaknesses. I didn't ask her to love me the way I was trying to love her, as a whole person, the good with the bad. I was loving her self-righteously rather than honestly, and I lost something in the experience. Or rather I missed out on an opportunity to find more of myself. If I had told Catherine how much she meant to me as a friend, if I had admitted how important it was to me to be considered "nice," perhaps she might have given me some of her own strength. She certainly had some, even if she used it in a negative way. And in the process I might have found that I could, indeed, put my feelings into words—which I didn't learn until much later.

## Loving with All We Are

When we love someone, we have to give that person our own need to be loved. We have to ask them to accept our faults just as we accept theirs. We have to invite them to care about what is happening in our lives. And we have to engage their strengths to combat our weaknesses. So we have to be honest about who we are and what we need. Loving is not the blanketing of the flawed by the one who is perfect; it is each one meeting the needs of the other so that they both can become their authentic selves. This is the goal of love; it is the basis of our relationship with God. We need one another, and we need all there is of one another.

We find it very hard to understand how God could possibly need us. From our point of view, God has everything—and who on earth are we to be so desirable? We forget that we are made in His image, that much of what we feel, He feels, too. Which is one of the reasons why He sent His Son to be as one of us. Christ had many needs, some we couldn't meet. He knew what it was to be lonely; He wanted someone to listen when He talked; He wanted a place to go and someone to go with; He could tell a good story and enjoy hearing one told; He liked to laugh and be in merry company; He wanted to accomplish something of importance; He wanted life to be better for those He loved. Yes, He needed us. Loving wasn't a favor He did for us; it was an exchange of needs.

And if the exchange is honest, it can't always be nice.

A woman I have known for a long time recently found herself doing something she couldn't stand seeing other people do. She was criticizing her husband in the presence of others. I had noticed it, too, and it made me uncomfortable when Janet would interrupt Lou and tell him to sit up straight and pull in his stomach. Lou never objected; he'd sit up straight and go on with his story, which was usually something in praise of Janet. Obviously Lou was proud of her, and I couldn't understand why that should annoy her. Frankly, it just didn't seem very loving—of her.

One evening when I was having dinner at their home, Lou announced that Janet, who was a nurse, had been made supervisor of her hospital nursing staff, an important and responsible job. "Usually they bring in someone from outside to take over," Lou said. "Janet's the first one from the staff to move up so high." He was beaming with pride.

Janet turned to him angrily. "Now that isn't true," she snapped. "There have been other supervisors who came up from the staff."

"But not as fast as you," Lou insisted, and I couldn't understand how he could hold his temper.

"No!" Janet said. "You're always giving me more credit than I deserve," she said, almost in tears. "And you don't give yourself enough. You're a wonderful teacher, and if you don't believe me, ask your students! But you talk about me as if I'm the strong one in the family. Well, I'm not, and if I'm going to take on this job, I'm going to need all the help you can give me."

Both of them forgot I was there, which was fine with

me. "Lou—I'm scared!" Janet said, reaching for his hand. "And I want it to be okay to be scared—and it isn't okay as long as you keep saying I'm so terrific!"

Lou was openly astonished. So was I. Janet had seen something in Lou that the rest of us had missed. He was holding back on his abilities because he thought they weren't good enough—and his doubts about himself were getting in the way of his own growth as a person. Janet's crankiness and her criticism were love's awkward way of coming to grips with a loved one's problem. Love, like God, can get very angry at times. But Janet was able to do what I couldn't do with Catherine: She offered to exchange weaknesses as well as strengths. And I think Lou accepted.

Back to the friend I'm afraid I'm going to lose . . .

Actually I have a choice. I can be quiet and try to keep the peace. I can tell myself that my friend has a childlike need to be reassured and that if I love her, I will either reassure her or keep my mouth closed. I can acknowledge that she does not want to change, take risks, or grow, and I can ask myself, Who am I to make demands she doesn't want to meet?

Nice—but not loving.

I would be meeting the needs of my friend's myth and not those of her person. I would be adding to the obstacles already in the way of her fulfillment. And I would not be keeping the peace between us; I would be keeping up the pretense that we love each other because—well, see how we get along together!

This time I am not going to stop loving. I am going to tell my friend how much I need what she gives to me: her thoughtfulness at those special times of the year when I need a family, and her generous sharing of hers with me; her sending me a get-well card every single day I am sick;

and her always being sure that something will work out well, even when it can't possibly. But more than that, there are other things I really need from my friend, and she has them to give: talking about the books we like, even though we rarely like the same ones; worrying about her children because we both love them, but for different reasons; sharing how we feel about our work because it's an important part of our lives, even though we'd never want to change places with each other. I need my friend's compassion, and that I know I can have. But I also want her communication, static and all, and I want her acceptance of mine.

I may not get what I want. I may not get anything. What then? What do I do with my love?

I keep on giving it, even if it isn't received. Because I will lose something vital to my life if I don't. The nature of love, as we know it, may be to withdraw in the face of rejection. But the spirit of love, as we learn it from God, is to stay, to wait, to hope—and to go on caring. To look for the slightest opening through which it can intrude itself into the life of the one it loves. There are others I love and others who will want my love, but I won't be able to give to them unless I realize how much there is in me to give.

Perhaps I will have to love in the way Catherine loved me a long time ago. And in the way God has always loved us all.

# 5

## But You Said You Would Always Love Me

I DIDN'T KNOW them well, but they seemed like two likable people. What was obvious, however, was their unhappiness with each other. She sensed that I noticed it, and one afternoon we talked. It was a story that is becoming painfully familiar.

They were married when they were quite young, and they grew apart. They began wanting different things out of life. She wanted excitement, he wanted serenity. He wanted another child, she wanted to explore a career first. Nothing wrong with any of their needs, except that they couldn't share the same ones, and they were uncomfortable with their differences.

That was a year ago.

Recently she wrote to me, and again the story was familiar. They were separated, and she felt a certain amount of relief from the tension of their marriage. She had a job, not what she really wanted, but it would do until she found something more challenging. He still didn't understand why she wanted to end the marriage and kept hoping she would change her mind. Her parents didn't understand, either. Some of their friends thought she was making a mistake. Sometimes she had doubts, too. She decided it was better not to see her parents or her friends or her husband for a while. They upset her too much. She was meeting lots of new people. One of them was a man—not just any man, but the man she had always dreamed of. He was everything she wanted, and the exact opposite of her husband. He understood her. They could talk for hours. They liked the same things. She realized it was too soon to get serious about someone, but . . .

I stopped reading. The letter might have been written by so many women I know, some of them older and married for more years, and each of them believing that what they needed most in life was a new and different person to make them feel comfortable. And the unhappy reality is that we have to make ourselves comfortable—with God. Are we becoming the persons God created us to be? And if we are, where do we go from there? Must we go alone?

*Love* is one of the first verbs we learn as speaking infants, and for a good reason. It connects us to the persons we need, and we gradually associate the words "I love you" with "I need you." As our basic young needs are cared for, we feel very warm and cozy and secure—we call it comfort. We and the people we love become each other's fulfillment, we maintain that baby-bunting level of comfort in each other's lives, and we are sincerely convinced that we cannot get along without it. Or without each other to provide it.

But if we begin to experience an ability to get along, even in small ways, without the one we love—*and* if that slight inclination toward independence makes us uncomfortable with that person—we assume that it means we no longer love each other. Because love and comfort go together, or so we think.

A certain amount of discomfort in love is unavoidable. As we get older, our needs become more complicated. We aren't as easily warmed, made cozy and secure, and we blame it on those we trusted to maintain that pleasant atmosphere. What we need, we decide, is the assurance that our changing needs are acceptable. We want someone to approve of the person we are becoming. In the meantime, those we love have been changing, too, and they blame us for not giving them the assurance they believe they need.

Can you appreciate what a chance God takes when He begins to love us? He starts early, when we are very new, not yet formed. Well, you may say, He knows what we're like and how we're going to turn out. But he doesn't.

He knows what we might become if we really work at it. But there aren't any guarantees. We have growing to do. We will change. We may start off well and then slow down. Or we may surprise Him with a sudden achievement in our later years. We may make very poor use—or none at all—of the abilities He gives us. Worse than that, we may not be comfortable with Him. We may think He doesn't understand us or our world. We may accuse Him of smothering us with love—or not loving us enough. We may refuse to live His way. We may stop loving Him altogether. Somehow He manages to go on loving us.

Do you suppose it may have something to do with the fact that God doesn't seek our consent to be who He is? And that He doesn't need our approval to be something other than what we want Him to be?

And do you suppose that we might find ways to go on loving each other, in spite of the changes in each of us, if we don't insist on being so comfortable with each other?

## To Be Is Not to Be the Same

What do we do when someone we love becomes someone we don't know? This is what happens throughout a marriage. No, we don't live happily ever after; we live in a state of constant change. That is, *if* the marriage is a sound one, and by that I mean a relationship between two people committed to enabling each other to become fully themselves.

Even if we think we know each other when we marry, we can't possibly foresee what each of us will become. We can't tell when or how often a change will take place, and we can't be sure we will like it. How ironic it is that so many of us are afraid marriage will become boring, when actually it is a history of surprises. The words in our marriage vows try to prepare us for some of them, but we are so preoccupied with claiming each other that we don't listen. We hear the cautionary phrases—we may not always have enough money, we may encounter times of hopelessness, we may not always be as healthy as we are. We nod vigorously, "Yes! Yes!"—but we have our whole life ahead of us and we know it will only get better. More money, more hope, more health—since we are already "everything!" to each other, we ask only to stay that way. Times may change, but we won't.

Nowhere in our vows do we promise to seek to know the persons we may become. Nowhere do we express our willingness to love what God wants each of us to be. And nowhere do we admit that if we grow into that potential, we may change in ways that make us less comfortable with each other. If someone were to add such considerations to the marriage ceremony, most of us would offer an unqualified "Yes!" But at such a time we know as little about loving as we do about each other.

Marriage is the closest relationship we enter into after leaving our parents, and even if we have been on our own for a time, we enter marriage as children. Each of us is seeking a parent because, to us, being close means depending on someone to take care of us. We expect marriage to be different from the relationship we had with our parents, yet we want it to give us the same assurances they gave us. And the realization that it *is* different, and not the same, changes us. We mark the occasion cynically: "The honeymoon is over." But it is over and it must be. Because we are not children and haven't been for some time. And because discovery is about to begin.

Who are we? And what can we give to each other? That is what marriage is all about. We cannot possibly know the answers ahead of time because it will take years of loving to find them. We are beginning to explore love as God loves: not knowing the outcome, but willing to open ourselves up to its possibilities.

"The honeymoon is over" means that we begin to see that we are not what we thought we were. We are concerned about more than each other. We concentrate on our work because it has become a serious matter: We are beginning to pay our own way in the material world, and the cost is alarming. We can expect it to go up—but will *we*? Will we get ahead, earn more, do more to earn more? Will we like what we do to get ahead? And if we don't, hadn't we better prepare to do something else now, before it's too late? We're not going to be young forever. Are we good enough to get ahead? What if we aren't?

(Yes, yes, I know you're there. I love you. It's just that I have these things on my mind. It's been a rough day. I'm beat. Sorry—I guess I didn't hear you.)

"Bill and I don't have that problem," a young woman named Sheila told me. She and Bill have been married for two years, and they knew from the beginning that each of them was going to concentrate on a career. "I understand how Bill feels when he comes home in a bad mood. I've been there. I can deal with it—and he can deal with me when it's my turn.

"It's later that I worry about. We both want children, but I'm not sure I want to be a mother. It would be such a big change—more for me than for Bill. We'd be so different. That scares me. I don't know how Bill would be as a father—or how I'd be as a mother. I suppose that sounds as if we don't know each other well. We do—but only as we are now. I wish we could stay that way."

But we can't.

Those of us who are young enough to choose whether or not to become parents will be changed by their decision. Women who choose not to have children will have greater opportunities to use their energies, their intelligence, and their experience early in their careers. They will satisfy those ambitions earlier. They will make room in their lives for risks; they will become more confident persons as they test their abilities and discover that they can learn as much from failure as they can from success. They may, at times, have doubts about the choice they made; an appealing child with caring parents may cause them to wonder if they were selfish—or self-denying. But one look at an unwanted child with troubled parents will confirm that the choice was the right one for them.

## Options Have Strings Attached

"I couldn't stand it if I had children the way my sister did," said a hardworking computer programmer married to a lawyer. "She's a good mother—don't misunderstand me. She's always there and she's up all night when they have colic or teeth coming in. But she and her husband and two kids live in an apartment that's too small for them, and they haven't got one dime toward a down payment on

a house. They're not even thinking about how they'll educate their children—because they know they can't.''

The young woman's sister doesn't seem nearly as worried. "I wanted children, and I wanted them while I was
young enough to do without a lot of sleep. We'll manage.
We'll have time for other things—later.''

Her choice was the more traditional one, and in that
sense her experience will be similar to that of many older
women. She already knows the pride, amazement, and
awe of bringing new life into the world. She has satisfied
that ambition. And for a long time, each day will hold a
fascinating new development in her child; the child will
grow and begin to be a person right before her eyes. She
will know, too, the responsibility of influencing so many
moments of her child's life, and she will agonize at times
because she will not always know the right thing to do.
She will take her share of risks. She will gain some confidence in her ability to keep a child healthy, to think quickly
in an emergency, and to come up with some incredibly deli-
cate explanations of how the world is put together—and
why.

She will know the peculiar alienation of being too long
in the company of children. She will ask too hungrily for
her husband to give her glimpses of what is going on in his
world. She will be tired, sometimes, from satisfying the
endlessly repetitive little needs of running a home—yet
she'll find them too trivial to describe without sounding
sour. But if you were to ask her what she does with all her
time, she'll tell you, and you may not like the way she does
it.

She may appear to know more about supermarket
prices than world affairs, but don't count on it. She keeps
up with the news. As she chauffeurs her children and sup-

plies her home, she has a lot of waiting to do—in small amounts. And she reads—everything she can get her hands on: magazines, novels, books about the world and where it's going and why it may not get there. This woman has a mind and wants to use it. Every now and then her husband, who may think she's lagging behind him, is startled by how much his wife knows.

She may not, however, consider her abilities to be of much value, especially when her children no longer seem to need them. She may long for some acknowledgment from the outside world that she can do something of value, and she wants a salary to prove it. But—she is still young. She has time to begin another kind of life. She'll get off to a late start; she'll be working for younger women who know much more than she does. And she'll be a little scared. She won't regret her choice to be a mother, but she may wish she had realized that she could be something else as well.

Some young women are hoping to avoid that melancholy reflection by choosing both motherhood and a career. Some other young women are not choosing it but are finding it necessary because the only way they and their husbands can have the children they want is for both parents to work. Either way, the choice has had its effect on the young men they marry.

I stopped for a school bus one day recently and saw four small children get out. Waiting for them were three men and a woman—at eleven-thirty on a weekday morning, that time when men used to be at work and women were looking after the children. The young mother and all three young fathers greeted their children with affection and enthusiasm, walking off in that wonderfully crooked stride of a big person holding the hand of a small person and asking, "What did you do in school today?"

I see men in laundromats, doing not only their own laundry but a family wash. And not grudgingly, but rather as something that has to be done and let's not make a big fuss about it. I see them in supermarkets, without their wives but sometimes with their children, shopping knowledgeably. Today's young fathers spend more time with their families; they don't find it demeaning to share the workload; they and the women they married know that they must share responsibilities in new ways. They have known it since they were children. They have learned it from watching their parents struggle to adjust to new pressures in the world. They knew they had to be different. The question is: Can they be flexible as they go on from where they are? Can they meet change any better than their parents could? We don't know. They have not had time to grow, to become someone less familiar to those they love. They have not been confronted with needs they didn't expect to have. They have not tried to live with the occasional discomfort that comes with becoming an individual.

They have not been caught, as their parents are, in the crunch between what used to be and what everyone can see is coming. In that sense, they may have some advantage.

## The New Woman and the Old Man

I surprised a younger woman by recalling a time when women were fired for wearing pants instead of a skirt to work. A friend who was an adult, as I was, during the early days of the women's movement now says of her twenty-two-year-old daughter, "She doesn't seem to realize how much opportunity she has—or how hard it was to get it for her. She seems so casual about it—I hope she can hold onto it."

She will. Opportunity, equality, identity, assertion—whatever you call it, it's part of a young woman's life today. Of course she can be at ease with it. It's those of us who were caught in the middle of change who are struggling to convince ourselves and those we love that we are still lovable.

Anna is only one of them—and there are many more. She and her husband, Cal, lived more or less the way their parents had lived. He worked, and she didn't. He reprimanded and praised their two sons and told them what was expected of them; she became part of their daily experiences. She had some money of her own, not much, but she didn't have confidence in her financial judgment, so she let Cal handle it.

She was an excellent hostess, and Cal often brought dinner guests home on short notice. Mostly business associates. He was proud of Anna, proud of their family, proud of their life. He praised her often and openly for helping him get ahead in his company. She was the perfect wife and mother. The only serious disagreement they had was when Anna, for a time, was a volunteer at the local hospital. She liked the work, had the patience for it, and would have given more of her time once the boys were in high school. But Cal liked knowing where she was. He complained that her work was taking too much of her energy and that his own career was feeling the loss of her interest in it. Anna quit. Life went back to normal.

Then there weren't as many dinner parties. Cal didn't travel as frequently, and he came home on time. He was as far up on the ladder of success as he had planned to go, which was high enough for him. He was a top executive in a large corporation, and his future finally was assured. He would stay where he was until it was time to retire, which he would do most comfortably. He was not an old man, but he was resting from running so hard. He had earned the right to it.

Anna, however, was feeling pretty good about herself. At first she missed the demands of being a hostess. It was one more thing gone out of her life, like the children who were now away more often than they were home. She was moving some of their possessions upstairs to the attic when suddenly she decided that the attic was too cluttered. Remembering that some of her friends had complained of the same condition, she called them and suggested they have a yard sale. Everyone agreed it was a great idea. Even Cal thought it was a smart way for Anna to make use of her time.

The yard sale was such a success that Anna and her friends were asked to help other women clean out their attics. They were only too happy to agree. They enjoyed the work and charged a percentage of the profits; the money wasn't much, but it gave them that lifting of the chin that comes from having monetary value in the world.

By the end of a year, Anna and two of her friends started a small consignment business. They rented a store and opened a thrift shop. At the end of the first month, when they found they had made enough money to pay the rent, with a little left over, they celebrated with a party at Anna's house.

Cal was noticeably withdrawn. Wasn't he feeling well?

He was fine.

Was he tired?

Why should he be? All he did was put in a day's work.

So did Anna. And on top of that, Anna took care of Cal. She made his breakfast, saw that his suits were cleaned, took his shirts to the laundry he preferred, even though it was on the other side of town, shopped for dinner, and then cooked it.

But there's dust on the tables. That never used to be. And the carpet needs vacuuming.

I can't do everything. Besides, nobody's here to see.

I'm here. But that doesn't seem to mean anything. All that junk you sell—is that all you care about?

It isn't junk! We don't take junk.

It might as well be. All you get is pennies for it.

You don't understand, Cal—they're *my* pennies! *I* earn them. And I like earning them. I like finding things that people can use. I like seeing them get excited because they find a plate that matches a dinner set they've had for years and can't use because too many plates are broken. I like seeing how excited people get when they find a bargain. And I like being smart enough to run a business.

I want you to give it up. I need a wife.

I can't give it up. I won't. (She almost said it—I don't need *you*—but something told her she really didn't mean it.) I'm still your wife, but I have to be more than that. I have to be—*me!*

Then be the *old* you!

Anna almost laughed out loud, except that she was too close to tears. Cal was the one who seemed old to her lately—and she felt wonderfully new. She had so much energy—and Cal was always so tired. She felt as if the best part of her life might be ahead of her, but Cal behaved as if the good years were done and gone.

It was true: Anna was winding up and Cal was winding down. Middle age does that to men and women, and Anna had read about it. She just didn't know how to deal with it.

Neither did Cal. Anna's enthusiasm and energy made him uncomfortable. He had worked hard to ensure that their later years would be filled with serenity, but Anna didn't seem to appreciate it. She was behaving like a kid, into all kinds of new things—pretty soon she'd want to try a new husband. Maybe a younger man, someone who could take her out to dinner instead of falling asleep in his chair. It was happening to some of his friends, and nobody knew why. One of them even went to a counselor, who explained why women were different from men at this age. But that didn't help. His friend felt the same way Cal did. He didn't want someone different. He wanted the woman he married.

Which is what he had. And Anna had the man she married. But they also had the persons they had become, and neither of them knew anything about these strangers.

The marriage wasn't necessarily over. But it was stale. It was at that much-publicized point where all kinds of aid can be suggested to bring a couple back to where they were in the beginning of their relationship. Nice try, and well intentioned—but it doesn't work. What Cal and Anna need is to go on from where they have been. They need to renew their acquaintance with each other—as they are now.

Angry as their exchanges have been, there is some truth in them. They don't need each other anymore—not, at least as they were when they were married. They have outgrown their immature selves, and they are able to meet most of their own needs on their own. But there is a great deal they can give to each other from the persons they have become, they are better able to love than they have ever been.

## Love Doesn't Play Roles

God has given us far more flexibility than we have learned how to use. We confine our love to stages and roles, and if it doesn't fit into the proper part at the proper time, then we think there is something wrong with it. Or with us.

Loving—as God loves—must be free to all things at any time.

I did not and never will outgrow my need for a parent. But I have one, and He is God. When I first realized that God was interested in me and in my life, I went running to Him as if I were a small child—which I was. I carried with me all my hurts and confusions about the world and the people in it. I went to Him for the understanding I couldn't seem to get from anyone else, and He gave it without question. He knew about the friends who could wound, the family that could divide, the dog who was killed by a car and the one I couldn't keep because a neighbor complained, the policeman at the school crossing who got sick and wasn't there anymore, the part of Snow White in the school play that I wanted so badly and didn't get. God, I thought, was Someone who could make things right—if He wanted to. And even if He didn't always right the wrong I presented to Him, knowing that He had that power made me feel good. In fact, I felt so well looked after that I began to attempt things I hadn't done before. It's part of growing, I know that, but in the process I wasn't the only one who changed. So did God. He didn't stop being my Father, but He also became my Friend, my co-adventurer. I could bring Him my fantasies about what I wanted to do when I grew up. He shared my disappointment when I learned that I wasn't cut out to become an actress; I'm much too methodical for such a spontaneous kind of life, and I'm inclined to sink roots wherever I go. I didn't tell Him at that point that I didn't think I'd be a good actress, either, because failure was hard for me to accept—but He knew. And I knew He knew. Just as He knew I would never become a veterinarian because as much as I wanted to help an animal, I couldn't deal with its pain. Those were experiences I didn't have to put into words, because God was right there feeling them with me. As I said, He was my Friend.

And like many good friends, we didn't always have much time for each other. I was busy getting an education and then wondering what to do with it, so I didn't get in touch with Him very often in those days. But when I did, He seemed to understand much more about the world than I expected. Once more I could bring Him the wrongs that I saw—the unkindness, the unfairness, the foolishness, the selfishness. He never told me I was young and idealistic and would get over it when I was older. He took me seriously. He showed me other wrongs—sickness, hunger, neglect, oppression, deceit. He showed them to me not as a Father, more concerned about the child than the student, but as one who thought I should know about such things because maybe there was something I could do to help. Apparently I had come that far; it was time for me to begin giving from what I had been given. I had grown up enough to love. Another change was occurring: We were becoming each other's partner. We didn't always succeed in what we tried to do, but we kept trying. That was important. Understanding what frustration could do to each of us helped to keep us going.

Us?

We?

How can I speak of God and me as if we were the same?

We weren't. We aren't. Not completely. Neither are you and I. Or you and anyone you love.

There are many things about God and me that made each of us uncomfortable. I was often too quick to move ahead. I grew, raspberrylike, taking over as much ground as I could cover, entangling with others, not taking time to acquaint myself with life's soil. I drew too much from it at times, asked for things it could not provide me. I was a scrawny, far-reaching plant with little fruit to show for my efforts. And God, although He never put obstacles in my way, kept nudging me to prune my busyness and take time to nourish my growth. He and I had to learn who we were—many times. We were never the same one day as we were the next; yet we were, each day, everything we had always been all the days we had known each other. We were at long last beginning to see who we really were.

I didn't always like the person I was becoming. And probably God didn't either. Not that I wanted to go on repeating mistakes I had made, but I didn't welcome what I had to do to avoid them. Such as looking out for my own well-being; and living up to what I said I would do, even in small matters I no longer thought were important; and speaking up for what I believed was right—in spite of those who thought I was wrong; and challenging what seemed to be false. I wasn't as soft a person as I thought I should be, but I didn't go running to my Father as often as I once did, asking, "What on earth am I going to do?" I spent more time conferring with my Partner, asking, "What's the best way for me to handle this?"

But I still have a Father, and there are times when I need what He can give me. No one else could understand how I felt when an automobile accident took the life of a young woman I had known and loved since she was two. And I am still troubled by friends who can hurt, especially when I am the friend who is doing the damage. I am still puzzled by this world and the way we live in it.

My Friend is still my Friend. I continue to tell Him about

my dreams for the future. I don't have as many now, and they are mixed in with a few fears because, after all, I am older now and more aware of what can happen to dreams. But He reminds me that my awareness of such hazards may enable me to come up with sturdier dreams.

God and I mean more to each other now because we know each other better. This is what happens in a close relationship, and especially in a marriage. But not without change, not without discomfort and occasional conflict, and certainly not overnight.

## Of Thee and Me

What happens when our needs collide with those of another? What do we do when someone close to us wants us to stop changing because change is uncomfortable?

We can't go backward. We can't allow someone other than God to create us, or to alter what He has begun. But— as we begin to explore our own hopes, as we seek our own talents and discover how to use them, we will stop asking the one we love to tell us we are wonderful. We don't need that anymore. We need to love.

As we begin to experience the satisfaction that comes from giving to another's needs out of the fulfillment of our own, we will know the real meaning of comfort: It is the joy of seeing someone we love become a whole person. We may not be able to meet all of a loved one's needs, but we can respect his or her right to have them. We don't need to be alike; we do need to be ourselves.

## Whoever You Are, I Love You

During the summer of 1984, while a much-celebrated athlete of astonishing speed and power was on his way to an Olympic gold medal, his wife attracted the attention of television interviewers who seemed to think that she was not your run-of-the-mill wife. She was deeply involved with her husband's achievements. She often ran with him in his daily workouts, she was the family business manager as well as the mother of their children; she understood the pressures her husband was under and sensed when it was time to talk or listen or find a reason to laugh.

"Well—do you ever get your roles confused?" one reporter asked her. "I mean, you have so many different relationships, do you ever forget you're husband and wife?"

The woman smiled and shook her head.

Her answer: "Sometimes we're brother and sister, sometimes we're business partners, and sometimes we're husband and wife. That's the way a marriage is."

It is—unless we imprison ourselves in roles, or stages, or myths.

What does it matter who cooks dinner? Or who goes out the front door in the morning? Or who has the patience and special understanding a child needs? Or who writes the checks? Or who makes more money? Those are some of the things we do, not who we are. And we can only love the persons we are, not what we do.

Why *can't* Cal slow down while Anna speeds up? Why *can't* Anna handle not only her own money but some of Cal's as well? If, at the end of the day, Anna is full of news about the thrift shop, why *can't* Cal enjoy listening to her— as she used to listen to him? Cal always wanted time to himself; there were books he never got to read, a few improvements he wanted to make in the house just to find out if he could do them; he has a secret longing to paint, although he knows nothing about art and isn't sure he has talent. Anna can understand such needs; she knows how satisfying it is to find something in ourselves we didn't know was there.

Marriage offers two people a unique opportunity to discover themselves and each other.

Will they be comfortable with each other?

Not always. That is, not if they continue to grow. And change. And offer to each other what God has given them.

# 6

## Please—Don't Turn the Light Out

I HAVE arthritic hands. My fingers are knobby in some of the joints, puffy here and there, and tend to stiffen in damp weather. Yet I can remember when a man I admired very much suddenly interrupted a serious, somewhat scholarly conversation to tell me I had graceful hands—and not to wave them around so much when I talked. My hands are far from graceful. But they do function. And quite well. I have been learning to train a young German shepherd dog who is very dear to me, and frankly I am amazed at the strength left in these stiff, odd-looking hands of mine. They hurt when they have to restrain this powerful animal from lunging at a squirrel across a busy road, but they manage to do what must be done.

So—what does this have to do with love? Quite a bit, I think. Especially the love of a parent for a child.

It is easy to love children when they are small. We have them under control, and we can tell ourselves that most of the threats to their happiness are in our minds. There is still time to solve their problems and make the way smooth for them—and for us. And smooth is the way we expect their lives to become—and they never do.

Why are we always surprised when children grow up

*into* problems instead of growing out of them? Why do we continue to believe the myth that when children reach the legal adult age, they no longer have any need of us? And why do we bristle so when they bring their agonies back home to us the way they once brought their scraped knees to be bandaged? Do you suppose it might be that a part of us feels like a child waiting for its chance to grow up? And that we might resent surrendering that chance to meet the needs of a child already grown and to whom we have given so much?

Just what do we do when our children return to the nest that has become pleasantly spacious without them?

## Whose Turn Is It? Theirs or Ours?

My closest friend is also someone I have known for many years, and recently we were reminiscing. When we were young wives, and her first child was a toddler, we would save up for a lunch together at a shopping mall. I used to marvel at her son's behavior; he could amuse himself with a few raisins and nuts and bits of lettuce from the salad bar while his mother and I dreamed dreams. She was a writer, too. Unknown, as I was, and hopeful, as I was. I think that, underneath all our wishful thinking about our future, we really didn't think it was going to be any different from that of our mothers. But we enjoyed savoring the possibility that it might.

A few weeks ago I was invited to a luncheon sponsored by a women's service organization. The only person I knew there was the woman who had invited me, and she was several years my senior. Because I think a lot of her, I accepted the invitation, but I didn't expect to be stimulated. I was in for a surprise. At a table with seven women I had never met before I found myself exchanging business cards

fifteen minutes after we sat down. My companions looked
like typical, middle-aged, suburban wives and mothers:
preppy-dressed, nothing overdone, and moderately up
with the times as far as issues went. They were anything
but. They were women finding out who they were and not
keeping it a secret. I never knew there were so many ways
a person could go into business for herself, but they were
educating me. The kids were gone, their husbands were
secure in their future—now it was their time. One thing
they had in common was their concern—and their
resentment—over their children. Too many of them were
coming back to roost.

"We had to postpone moving into a smaller house,"
one woman said. "Both my son and daughter are back with
us—but it's not the way it used to be. For some reason, I
feel crowded."

"I do without a lot of things so I can afford to help my
son pay for his own apartment," another said. "I've been a
mother long enough. I'm here if he needs me—but I'd
rather not have him live with us. I don't have the patience."

"I hated it when my kids left home"—this from another
mother—"but I got used to it. I was just beginning to enjoy
my own freedom when—bang!—back came the kids. I
don't understand them. We gave them everything they
needed for a wonderful life. Why aren't they happy? And
why can't they live their own lives? We did!"

It's a familiar cry: *I love my kids—but now it's time to love
myself.* And who can blame you if that's the way you feel.
After all the hard work, the giving, the taking what you
didn't always want to receive—at last you have everything
the way you want it.

Yet there are these others for whom you put aside your
own needs for so long. And they want—more!

No! You've given enough. Let them take care of themselves. You can't give any more.

But you can.

What about your peace and quiet? What about your security, that comfortable little assurance about the future? That bit of money in the bank? And the time you call your own? A few more wrinkles on your brow? A few more gray hairs? A little less sleep? You have all that to give.

Can we really live without caring? Without caring *about*? We aren't meant to, you know.

There is very little, if any, need in this world for someone who has no obligations to anyone else, no responsibility for the well-being of another, and no demands on her time other than her own choice of what to do with the rest of her life. If this is the way we are going out into the world, then we are not properly qualified to work in it. Because anything that needs to be done will require the ability to give of ourselves, to put something or someone ahead of us, to juggle what we want out of life with what we must put into it.

Leave all these valuable credentials behind, and we have nothing to offer that the world really needs.

I can only imagine what God must feel when I keep coming back to Him in tears, I who am far beyond the normal years of childhood. Granted, He is God, but since I am made in His image, I have some inkling of His sensitivities. And I must allow Him a certain amount of annoyance at my frequent reappearances on His threshold. I say "allow Him" because He never reveals anything but patience and a willingness to try to understand why I need Him so desperately. There are other times when He senses more quickly than I do what is troubling me and helps me to reach that perspective.

I don't think my never-ending need for God prevents

Him from being God. If anything, it confirms who He is. Because in the very act of creating me, God made me a promise to be there—and by *there* I mean *in my life*—at all times. If He were to go back on His promise because I am older now and should be able to take care of myself, then He wouldn't still be God. And I think the same is true of a parent. We can't erase the fact that we are a parent. We are stuck with it—or blessed with it—depending on how we look at ourselves. And once we cease being a parent to a child, then we are no longer who we truly are—no matter how much time we have left to develop ourselves.

## When Do You Stop Being a Parent?

Never.

What do you get out of it?

Ask God. He doesn't want anything in return for all He gives us. Yet the very fact that we exist seems to bring Him pleasure. And pain as well.

I have never wondered whether God had something better to do with His time than to look after me. Or simply to be there when I need Him. Am I ungrateful? Selfish? Irresponsible? No. I am His child. So are you. You and I and the Son He already has and has given—we have first claim on Him.

As our children have on us. Not only until they are old enough to get a job and start a family of their own. Always. They change, yes, but so do parents. As we grow, we don't part company with our children. We meet their different needs in different ways.

A psychologist I know made a simple statement that gave me a lot to think about: "Adolescence, these days, lasts at least until the age of thirty." He wasn't speaking cynically, but rather with compassion for both parents and their physically mature children. He was saying that life isn't the same as it was when you and I were young, Maggie. But then you and I have heard that before, haven't we? From our children.

We've heard it, but we may not have understood it.

That is not a familiar world out there, so we can't know how it feels to live in it. We approach it carefully, with an inquiring toe, but we can retreat to a warmer environment if the waters make us shiver. Our children can't. They can only come home. For a while. They know they will have to leave again. Many times, perhaps.

Why?

Not because someone—they or we—did something wrong. Not because we gave them too much or too little. They were well prepared to survive, to excel, to surpass— but in a world that no longer exists. We equipped them for our world, for the one our parents and their parents knew, and it isn't there anymore. We don't know what is required in our children's world because no one has lived there long enough to draw conclusions about it. Our children will have to find out for themselves, and that will take time.

How do you live in a world without guidelines? As much as we resented the ones we had, as unfair as many of them were, they spared us a lot of decisions. We didn't always follow them scrupulously; we didn't always do the right thing; but if we missed more than a few guidelines, we found ourselves quite alone in the world. And we didn't enjoy it. Guidelines, and the observance of them, didn't necessarily make us better people; but they kept us where almost everybody else was, and we felt safe. We didn't ask whether something was right just because everyone did it; we assumed it was. We still do. We don't like to have our ways questioned; it makes us uneasy. We don't want to decide so many issues for ourselves.

The way our children do. And must.

A middle-aged man who always took his father's advice was telling me what a disappointment his daughter is to him. Halfway through college she wanted to drop out and get a job. Travel, maybe. "It was a good school," her father said. "Not too demanding academically, but she was the one who picked it out. She wanted the social life, and there was plenty of it. Then she decided she was wasting her time and not learning anything." She didn't leave, because she realized how much it would upset her family. She graduated with respectable grades, although she wasn't interested in her courses.

"And then," her father said, shaking his head, "I got her a job through a friend who's a banker—and she wouldn't take it!"

Did she want to work in a bank? "No, not especially," he said. "But she won't need a job for long. She'll fall in love and get married and have a family—so what difference does it make where she works?"

It was very hard for this very caring man to see what his daughter had to confront: Having a family did not mean that she wouldn't also work. Doing one or the other was typical of our world; in our children's world it's a luxury few will be able to afford. And if you're going to work for the rest of your life, you had better do something you like.

"She's gone out West," he said. "She's working in a resort out there—because she likes the weather." He was painfully confused. In "his" day—ours, too—people didn't make decisions about the weather. They put up with it. His daughter may decide to do the same thing—or she may decide to get the training she needs to do the kind of work she enjoys in the climate she prefers. But that, too, will take time.

"I'm still waiting to be a grandmother," a friend says.

Her son didn't marry right away—"He was almost thirty!" And now, a few years later, still no sign of children. "What are they waiting for?"

To see if the marriage will last? To forecast whether they can afford to have, care for, and educate a child? To ask themselves, honestly, whether they want to be parents?

"We didn't even know there were such questions," my friend said sadly. "Maybe we were better off."

Maybe. Maybe not. We can't know, and it isn't important that we do. We may never understand the world our children live in, but we do have to understand *them*. And the only way we can gain insight is by loving them.

But—that's what you've been doing all these years!

No. You haven't. You have brought up your children. You have provided them with more than the necessities of life. But you couldn't possibly understand them, because they were in the shadow of your authority. You were responsible for them. Now they are becoming responsible for themselves. They are becoming what God created them to be. And you have to get to know them as if you had never met them before. Now you have the opportunity to learn *how* to love them.

Since we aren't exactly like God, only partly, we cannot be there in the life of a child at all times. But, like my knobby fingers, we can still function. We can be the parent a child can go to. Whenever.

If ever a Child grew up in a world very different from the one He had known with His Parent, it was Christ. And even in His adult years among us, He needed to spend some time away from the company of strangers. He went to the One who was known: to God. And He did it through prayer. Our children come home for the same reason. They need sanctuary. It's something no one tells us about in the earlier years of bringing up a child, in the days when so much physical care is required, because that isn't when it's needed. Sanctuary is something only a grown parent can give to a grown child. And it asks of us not only what we may not want to give, but what we may not realize we have. Time, space, warmth, continuity—these are sanctuary.

## More than the Ticking of the Clock

The time our grown children need from us now is not a matter of minutes or hours, but a single moment. *This* moment. More specifically, does this moment belong to them—or to us? Never mind how many other moments have been theirs. Is *this* one theirs? Do their needs come before ours *at this moment?* Or at any moment?

I cannot believe that God, my Father, would answer no to these questions. Or that any of us could say no—without losing the best parts of ourselves.

You and I, especially because we are women, want to get to where we think we ought to be. And as quickly as possible. There is nothing wrong with that, and God has certainly given us the ability to move in that direction. But it *is* a direction, and not all of us will be able to reach our goals in our lifetime. We may be delayed, sidetracked. Some of us may have to decide whether we are willing to help another go a little farther—and let it go at that. It doesn't mean we stop growing; it means we grow in ways we didn't plan.

Some of us may be confronted with a difficult question: Are we willing to lay down our lives—in the sense that we put aside our own ambition—so that others can move farther ahead? It's not a radical idea; some of our own parents have done it because it was the thing for parents to do in their day. Today we have a choice. We know that time does not belong to our children. This moment is not necessarily theirs. It is what they *ask* of us—and rightly so, because they are our children—but we have a parent's right of refusal.

So did God. So did Christ.

We don't have as much time as our children do. If we claim this moment as our own, is it so terrible?

No.

Except that what we do with this moment is more important than how long the moment may last. Our choice will shape the kind of person we become, and the way we are able to love. If we claim the moment, if we hold on to the time we know is ours, we will grow in strength and determination. And these are good qualities. If we yield to our children's need, if we give them our time, or a portion of it, we haven't lost our sense of direction. We haven't deprived ourselves of fulfillment. We are, instead, providing a path for others to travel—to where we hoped to go. And we will grow in love.

### The Right to Be—In Our Midst

Children at any age take up space, and most would rather have a room of their own. But that isn't the kind of space a sanctuary offers. The family nest, once emptied, may have shrunk; its location may have changed. We may have to squeeze a returning child onto a sleep sofa in the living room. Or give up our hopes for a guest room at last. Or that den where we had been able to work undisturbed, our papers and tools spread out around us. We will not be comfortable, and neither will the child who returns. Angry confrontations over minor privacies and territories will inevitably occur. Ignore them. Argue if you must, and feel free to express yourself. Inconvenience is not important here.

What counts is the space you are able to give your adult child to be and to become himself. It has nothing to do with inches.

These are not infants or teen-agers coming back into your living quarters. They are grown human beings seeking time away from pressures that are trying to force false identities on them. They know better than to say "Yes, I will be what the world wants me to be," but they feel alone in their insistence that they have a right to become the people God wants them to be. They wonder, at times, if anyone else agrees with their vision of themselves.

You know very well how that feels. Your world is a different kind of place, but you have come to that same point in it. Of all people, *you* are not at odds with these adult children of yours. *You* can understand their anxiety—better, possibly, than anyone else. Your understanding is the kind of space they need.

Can you give it to them?

Can you give them the freedom to determine their own life—even while they are living in your house? Can you resist being the mother you once were to the infants they used to be? Can you become the adult parent they need?

Can you give serious attention to their concerns about their world? And can you resist minimizing these concerns because you are, after all, their parent and you feel you must offer some kind of reassurance that the world isn't as bad as they think it is? Can you honor their solutions to their own problems and encourage them to persist in them?

Can you confront the behavior that you don't like without threatening to withdraw your love if the behavior isn't changed? Can you respect their differences of opinion?

Their perception of values where you see none? If there are rules in your house, are some of them theirs? And do you observe them as respectfully as you do your own and those of the other members of your family?

All this is space.

## Until the Chill Is Gone

When your children were small and went out to play in the snow, sometimes they stayed too long. When they came home in response to your calls, you could see how cold they were and you held them close to you. It was the fastest way you could warm them, because you were the source of what they needed: You were the life-sustaining energy, and you felt good giving it. If you have ever clasped the snow-cold hands of a child between your own, you know that you really didn't lose your own warmth; you increased it by transmitting it to another. You remember the life-giving sensation of feeling your child's hands recover their own warm suppleness. You had loved the small fingers back into motion, and they gave warmth to you as they curled around your hand.

Your children, now grown, still need your warmth. But in a different form.

The world has chilled your children severely by making demands on their judgment. They have had to evaluate morals, principles, behavior—their own and that of others—without benefit of guidelines, and without time to gain experience in making judgments. They have constantly been challenged to question what they believe is right and wrong and in Whom they believe. The confrontations may have taken the energy—the heat—out of their determination to go on.

You can help.

You have judgment. You have lived longer than your children have. You have known the experience of being right and being wrong—and being mistaken about one thing or the other. You won't evaluate your children's world in the same way they do, but the fact that you take stands in your own world means something. You have been warmed by doing what you believe is right; you have been warmed by opposing what you believe is wrong.

You can't give your convictions to your children. They have to form their own. But you can give them the energy you have gained from using your judgment; you can put back into their determination the warmth the world has taken from it.

You and your grown children will not always believe in the same things. Or in the same ways. Your children also haven't had time to test what they believe, and as they do, their beliefs will change. Often. They will need warming— often. It will be a long time before their own judgment is practiced enough, and strong enough, to make sense out of what is going on in their world.

Your children have a right to find God in their own way. And God has a right to find your children in their own world. They will form their own relationship. But until the chill of their confusion is gone, you can give them the warmth of your belief that it is important to believe. And if you can do that, then God can love your children through you.

## You Can Leave the Door Open

From the time I was twelve years old, I carried a set of house keys. Both my parents were at work every day, and the keys meant that no one was home. The cost of hiring someone to look after me had become too high—and, besides, I was old enough to look after myself. Like many children today, I got along very well.

But I would hate to think I had to use a key to be at home with God. I want to know that His door is always open. Our grown children feel that way about coming home, they just want to walk in and make contact with the other lives there. They need to know that they have been missed, and that they have a place in the thoughts and the hearts of those they love. They don't want to be locked out; they don't want to have to use a key to get back in.

They want continuity—which is a little bit of what we all get out of a family reunion, if we are fortunate enough to have one.

Continuity is the realization that there is more to life—and to ourselves—than what we are experiencing at the moment. It's a sense of ongoingness, a feeling of connection between our lives and those that have gone before and will come after. It is as close as we can come to immortality while we are yet mortal.

Continuity is what you give your children when you allow them into your life again. It's more than understanding who they are; are you allowing them to discover who *you* are? As much as you give to your children, even after their return, are you asking *of* them to meet your own needs? They can. They haven't come home for a handout; they have brought themselves, and they are much more than the children who went away. God has had time to create more of them. They are learning, as you still are, how to love, and there is much you can give to one another.

Let's not forget something. Our children aren't the only ones who need to come home now and then. We all do. We all need sanctuary from the stresses of life, and we want to know it's always there.

But where?

Home isn't a place. It's knowing we belong. It's where the sharp angles and rough edges of our individual selves somehow manage to fit in with the angles and edges of others to form a whole. Home is made up by each person who is a part of it, and we are only really home when each person is present. Not actually present, in a physical sense. But present through the relationships we form when we truly love one another.

So—you might say that when our grown children come home, it enables us to come home, too.

# 7

## I Thought They Would Always Be Young

I CAN'T GO HOME AGAIN—at least not to a place. The house where I grew up is still there, but a different family inhabits it. My parents live in a retirement community. Oh, it's a very nice one, and as long as they are careful, they won't have financial worries. I guess you could say that my parents are comfortable. It's just that I'm not.

I don't know how to relate to my parents. It shocks me to see them changing physically, almost in front of my eyes while I'm visiting them. My mother always looked young for her years. Her skin was smooth and unlined—until yesterday. Yesterday she had wrinkles. A lot of them. My stepfather used to be an athlete. Now he shuffles when he walks.

Our conversations are awkward. Their interests are in their immediate neighbors. The most important part of their day is the dinner menu in the glass-enclosed dining room overlooking the man-made lake, where a family of ducks glide across the water. My world is so different. I worry about making my living. I wrestle with a chapter that won't come out on paper the way I hear it in my head. I am concerned about a friend whose marriage is in trouble. World conflicts threaten me—my opinion about who is right and who is wrong shifts, and there is much to debate. But not with my parents. What can we talk about?

I'm not prepared for this. Being a child of God isn't the same as being a child of human parents who grow old. I panic when I realize that I can't pick up the phone and know that my parents will help me solve a problem. Not that I called on them often in the past, and not that I always took their advice. But they were *there*, and that made a difference. I felt as if something were undergirding me.

Now, seeing my parents' frailty, I feel that *I* must do the undergirding. *I* must tell *them* what is best for them to do. I must tuck them in to sleep for the night.

But I don't want to become the parent of my parents. I don't want to treat them like children. I can't. And I shouldn't.

Something is coming between us, making it hard for me to love them. I want to put them aside, not visit them as often. I am angry at them for aging, for leaving me in favor of a family of ducks. They are so insulated in their scheduled community; I am so open to siege. I am so frightened.

Of what?

Of time, and our inability to halt it. Of the end of life and what I don't really know about it. I don't want my parents to age because *I* don't want to age. Yes, there it is, out in the open: I don't want to see where my parents are going because eventually I will walk there, too.

I was mistaken. God has indeed prepared me for this time. He prepared His own Son for mortal life by placing Him in the care of a man and a woman very much like my parents. Or yours. Perhaps it was His way of teaching His immortal Child that life here changes swiftly. And that we must not allow these changes to sweep away the relationships that keep us from being pulled under by the fast-moving currents. This truth is as valuable to me as it was to Christ.

No, I am not the parent to my parents. I am still their child. And I must not mistake their fragility, or the lightness of their bones, or the occasional fatigue of their memories for a return to childhood. They have been there and they are far beyond it now.

What does my mother feel when she looks in the mirror and finds there a sudden stranger? What will I feel when it is my turn? She can tell me, without speaking a word—if I am willing to hear her. What can my stepfather tell me about a body that no longer leaps to the mind's commands? He can show me how to soften my gait—to a shuffle, perhaps—to ease the stress on it. My stepfather gets where he needs to go. (I must say, I don't always.)

This man and this woman are not easy for me to love— because it isn't easy for me to face my own fears of what lies ahead of me. But if I do not put false labels on them, if I do not call them "child," but, instead, "father" and "mother," then my hand will still be in theirs, and my own fear will begin to subside. I need them now more than ever. They can help me to prepare for the problems I have yet to meet.

## Time Is Not an Enemy

When I was growing up, my stepfather's father was the only grandfather I knew. My mother's father and my father's father had died rather early in life, and I hardly remembered them. But Grandpa Jim, as I called him, was a definite presence in our home, even though he didn't live with us. Actually our relationship with him was somewhat formal in that we visited him on certain holidays and special occasions, and he bestowed himself upon us three times a year: Christmas, Easter, and the Fourth of July. Believe me, his presence lasted from one of those days to the next.

Grandpa Jim was a tall, heavyset, handsome man with steely gray hair and scowling dark blue eyes—the perfect grandfather to make children sit up straight. He had a deep, raspy voice, which he cracked like a bullwhip to keep all of us, adults as well, in line. He liked to be treated as if he were a king, and we did exactly that. We enjoyed doing it.

We weren't fooled by him and his harsh voice and his furrowed brows. We knew that after dinner, where he always overate, he would settle into the softest chair and pretend to be listening to what we were saying. He would nod slowly, which gave the impression that he was taking everything in; actually he was falling asleep, which he did quite gracefully. His big gray head would tilt to one side as his eyes closed gently. He never snored and his mouth never fell open. He was quite dignified. But a change always came over his face when he was sleeping: The sternness vanished, and instead there was an expression of sweetness. That's why I say he didn't fool us: He was a softy.

But at the dinner table, he was a tyrant, and I resented him. He was always given first choice as to the part of the holiday turkey he preferred, and it was always the same: the drumstick and second joint, with a few slices of white meat from the breast. Not unusual for a grandfather, of course, but I used to wish that just once he would ask if anyone else wanted the other drumstick and second joint. We all knew he would finally end up with both of them, so there was no point in anyone else choosing those parts. To cover my resentment, I would ask for a wing, which I bit into as if it were the most luscious treat on earth.

At our first holiday dinner after Grandpa Jim died, we were at a loss. No one, it seemed, wanted a drumstick or second joint. Until it was my turn. When I was offered them I accepted. I ate them, too, but I didn't enjoy them. Not that I felt I was taking something that didn't belong to me. My problem was that I felt totally unprotected. Grandpa Jim, all big and demanding and deep-voiced, wasn't standing between me and time anymore. That's why no one else wanted his parts of the turkey. It was the reason why my stepfather was ill at ease sitting at the head of the table. In a way it was like moving forward in a line that was waiting to get to the end of something.

I am much farther ahead in line now, and my parents are up ahead of me. The line doesn't always inch forward in an orderly fashion; some of us move forward abruptly, ahead of many others. But that isn't typical. Usually time is something we can see, in terms of the people we know who are getting older. And how exuberant we are when we meet someone we haven't seen for a long time and he or she doesn't look that much older. "You haven't changed a bit!" we exclaim, hoping to hear something similar in reply. Of course it isn't true. Some of us age more quickly than others, or more noticeably at certain periods in life. But we all age. Every minute. Every hour. Time does not pass us by.

Time is not meant to torment us, but rather to give our love an opportunity to adapt itself to our new needs. Time is not the end of what we are, but a reminder that we have other places to go, that other changes will occur—to us, to those we know and love, to the world, and to beyond the world.

Our parents are living longer than they expected they would. Consequently they are taking up residence in a world that is just beginning to be populated. They aren't prepared for it anymore than our children are for theirs. Most of our parents won't live out their days in the house they paid for in their more vigorous years. They may not be able to afford the taxes on it, or the second mortgage they took out to give their children an education. They may not be able to keep the house neat and in good repair because, while their minds may be sharp, their bodies will lose agility. They may sell what they own and move to a retirement community where they can let someone else worry about shoveling and mowing and medical bills. But who knows how long they will be able to pay for the monthly maintenance of their guaranteed peace?

Very few of our parents will live out their days in a rocker on the front porch. Many of them will decide what their last day will be by requesting release from the tubes and mechanisms of a hospital chamber.

## Coming of Age

It was so simple. A little after lunch a neighbor called me from work. Her daughter was running a temperature, and the school nurse had called. Would someone come for Maryanne? Her mother was at a meeting; my schedule was more flexible. Of course, I'd be glad to. I was there in ten minutes. I brought my dog along to make Maryanne smile. Then I dropped her off at her home, where she went straight to bed.

Later, when her mother called to thank me, I interrupted. "Don't," I said. "It was something I wanted to do. Maryanne means a lot to me—and so do you."

It was such an easy way to love.

But ask me to spend an afternoon with my aging mother and I will try to find a way out of it. I can talk to Maryanne about anything; she is interested in me, in everyone. My mother and I find it hard to talk; we're preoccupied with our own fears. Time ticks very loudly when we're together.

Loving our children, even when they are grown, is easier than loving our parents when they are old. Children are new life, traveling areas where we once walked, and even if they strike out on different paths, we can look back fondly over where we have been. Nostalgia is a sweet perfume, reminiscent of fresh-cut flowers and yellow-green leaves. The past is a safe place to recall because it is over and done with; we can't change what happened to us there, but neither do we have to wonder what to do. It has already been done.

Aging parents are old life, and there is an acrid scent among the dried blossoms. Some withering is present; the colors are paler. But more than that, it is a place where we must eventually go, and we don't know our way around it. It is as alien as the world of our children, but we don't have any choice about whether or not to enter it. We must.

But in what way will we enter it? As infants crying out against the darkness? Or as adult children who can share a meaningful season with those they love?

The parents who need us now, need us as adults who can recognize that they, too, are adults. Which means that we must finally give up whatever remains of our childhood. Little children can't deal with the end of things—or even the beginning of some; adults can. Little children resist change; adults explore it.

But how does one grow out of childhood?

That, too, is something love can teach us. If we are willing.

The men and women Christ left on a dark and dusty road the night He was arrested were children. He had done what He could to educate them in the ways of maturity, and there had been some progress. Yet they remained childlike. They wanted to be cared for—not because they were selfish or heartless, but because they felt too weak to bear anyone else's burden. For who were they?—nobodies. And, like us, they vowed many marvelous things, but they knew in their hearts they were only speaking words. They did *not* want to grow stronger or wiser or more sensitive— partly because they had no idea where such developments would take them.

When, a few days later, a resurrected Christ spent some final hours on a quiet beach with some of those same peo- ple, they weren't children anymore. They had grown into adult companions who could share what was happening to Someone they loved.

What made the difference? What accounted for their growth? Shock? Terror? Remorse? They had suffered all those things, but that wasn't what changed them.

They had been loved out of being childlike. They had seen, on a cross-marked hill in the worst part of town, how very much love could care and give to them. And being so loved convinced them of their value. They became aware of their own strength, of their own ability to give, to bear pain if necessary and still to go on loving. They could face their own fears and whatever else life presented to them. They had grown up.

And when we grow up, we can look life straight in the eyes. We can end our war with time and begin to appreciate where it takes us. Wherever we are, at whatever age, we will find ways to love.

I can't be old for my aging parents. My time will come. But I can walk alongside them in their sparsely populated new world. I can help them settle there. I can't end their fears, but I can share them, and I think that makes a difference. I can also observe and begin to imagine how I will meet that time of gentle loosening of my grip on the life I know—and my somewhat anxious expectation of the one I do not. And by understanding what *I* might need at such a time, I can perhaps meet my parents' needs.

## Don't Count Me Out

If I were old, I would want my place at the table. I might not always be there, and I certainly won't mind if someone sits in my chair when I am away. But it should be *my* place; it should speak of who I am and what I mean to the others around the table. Don't put my name on it—nothing as impersonal as that. Just know that I am there, or if I am not, that I would like to be.

And when I'm there, please know who I am. Don't put food on my plate for me if I can serve myself. If I'm clumsy, serve me as you would serve yourself—simply, without interrupting your conversation, or your silence. I don't need to be told that food is on my plate. I know how to eat, but I came for more than that. I'm here to be with you. I'm here because I need you to want to be with me.

I may cause you some inconvenience; we old ones are like that. Can you accommodate it? Can you put my needs ahead of yours, even though they are different from yours?

Christ had a way of rising to the occasion—of changing water into wine and feeding an unexpected multitude with a few leftovers. Can you do that for me—of course, on a much smaller scale?

But think about it: What did it matter to Christ that it was only water a young couple's parents could afford to serve at a wedding feast? It didn't.

But it mattered to some people He loved. And He was able to give Himself to their needs. Water became wine.

If I am old, then I am concerned about things you can't understand. Because you don't need them. This is why you and I can't talk freely these days. You can make do with water—but I need wine.

I am set in my ways—this is my wine. I cannot change as easily as you can because I have less time in which to adapt to something different. And I cannot make the wine to meet all my needs anymore. Yet the needs are still there. Will you help me to fill those vessels?

When I was younger, and as I was leaving a wedding ceremony in the company of two dear and much older friends, I didn't notice that my friend on the right was slowing down. His wife, who was on my left, did. "Put your arm through his," she whispered softly to me. "*Don't* lift him up!" she cautioned. "Let him lean on you—if he wants to."

And I realized then what a difference it makes to put our strength where someone can use it, at will, instead of pressing it on him. When I slipped my arm through Herb's, his pace increased slightly, but he never gave me a glance. My help was there for him to use as he chose. It was a lesson I was grateful to learn, and I have made good use of it many times since. I think Herb's wife learned it from loving him.

And it's what I would like from you because you love me: Give me the help I need to help myself. And let me take as much or as little as I need.

## A Room of My Own

If I were old, I would want to go on being the person I am, and you should have the same right.

Allow me to change, but don't try to change me. I am still growing, however slowly. Don't get in the way of it. Please. This is important to me. It's as if God gave me something to take care of all these years, and I don't want to let it go.

For instance, don't assume that I want to move in with you and your family. Or that I want to live in a community of people my age. Let me be a part of that decision.

Don't try to make me over to accommodate your needs. Or your fears.

As a child I lived across the street from my best friend. Her name was Nancy, and since I spent many afternoons at her house, I knew her family quite well. Nancy's father was a real homebody; he was *the* photographer in town, and his studio took up half of their house. He was always home for lunch, which was something new for me because most fathers were away all day. Nancy's mother, on the other hand, was rarely home; she was a crusader, a do-gooder, a fixer-upper. She was or had been the president of every women's organization and she took her work seriously. Mostly I remember her coming out the front door as I was going in, calling out instructions to Nancy about setting the dinner table and worrying out loud about how she was going to attend two meetings being held at the same time. And, oh, yes, how are you, dear, and why don't you stay for dinner? She always seemed upset and in a hurry, and I used to hope that someday she would find time to stop and rest.

Nancy and I remained good friends, but we didn't see each other often after high school. We went to each other's wedding, but after that we lived far apart. We wrote to each other about husbands, children, making ends meet. We rarely mentioned our parents. Until one day Nancy telephoned me long-distance and asked me to visit her father, who was a patient in a Veterans Administration hospital near my home. He had suffered a stroke.

I'll never forget that visit. Or the sight of what happens to a man who loves his home and can't be in it. Or the way he cried from loneliness when he remembered who I was and what his life had been.

The family really didn't have a choice. They didn't have much money and they decided that the most important need was proper medical care, which Nancy's father certainly was receiving. But red tape being what it is, he was assigned to a hospital far from any members of his family. He died not long after I saw him.

Many years later, Nancy and her husband and three children moved back to my neighborhood, and we began to see more of each other. Her mother lived with them, and Nancy was very proud of the room and bath that had been especially renovated to give her privacy and a sense of independence. The family had been quite successful, and money was no longer a problem. But Nancy remembered how her father had suffered from being away from home and she wasn't going to let that happen to her mother.

I barely recognized Nancy's mother sitting quietly in a Barcalounger in front of a color TV set. It wasn't a physical change as much as it was the attitude of the woman. I had never seen her sit still before. Her eyes had always been filled with expression—even if it was a worried one—but now they were fixed. She wasn't watching the TV screen; she wasn't watching anything. She had lost interest in life. She was getting the best of care, but she was a woman who lived and drew her energy from *giving* care.

Nancy took it as a personal defeat when her mother's doctor insisted that she be sent to a nursing home. He said she needed the kind of supervision a family couldn't possibly give. Nancy felt she was doing the wrong thing, but she did it. She cried for hours after she left her mother in the care of strangers. She visited every day, ready at her mother's slightest indication of unhappiness to take her back home.

The indication never came. Within a few weeks, Nancy's mother was deeply involved with crusading, doing good, and fixing up whatever could be improved at the nursing home. She formed committees and ran them; she gave other patients a new interest in their lives; she was known and liked by patients and staff members—and the most remarkable thing was that her own health was immensely improved. What she had needed for so long was the chance to go on being her authentic self instead of the little old lady her very loving daughter wanted her to become.

Nancy couldn't argue with the results. "How wrong can you be?" she said.

Very. Especially when we think in terms of age instead of the person.

## Being Here

If I were old, I would not want to be alone. And that can happen, whether I move in with you or live somewhere else.

You and I, each of us, are alone if we cannot share each other's world.

I have been in yours, but you hesitate to enter mine. You keep calling me back to your world, not realizing that I cannot return. You are the one who can come to me. And I wish you would. We need each other's love.

Even though I find difficulties in my world, even though I can't answer some of my questions about what will happen to me here, it is a world that accommodates me. I don't have a lot of time left in my future here with you, but I *do* have time in the present to see and do what you cannot do. Knowing I can't move as quickly as I once did, I think a bit longer about what I am going to do. And in my times of reflection I am discovering a spiritual fitness: I'm not ignoring you or your concerns by watching ducks on a pond; I am humbled by the knowledge that God also watches them. And that He watches me. And you. I am moving closer to His world than to yours, perhaps—but that is where I belong.

Nevertheless I am here. Be here with me. Let me show you what is good in my world, since you already know what is disturbing. If you have taken me into your home, don't keep me out of your life. If I choose to live with others and in another place, come and spend time with me. I don't keep the same pace you do, but we have never felt the need to be identical. If I don't solve your problems in the way you want them solved, there is nothing new about that. We haven't always agreed on what is important.

Come be my child who is grown. Let me see what my life has meant in yours. Let me go on loving.

## I Am Where I Have Been

I have a brush-and-ink sketch that no one else thinks is beautiful. And probably it isn't. But I bought it years ago because I saw something else in it. It's a drawing of trees, in winter: no leaves, an abandoned nest high up in one of them, frozen snow on the ground. And to me there is nothing sad about the scene. The trees are strong, still graceful although somewhat bent by the pressures of living. In their clean, stark branches and gray-barked trunks I see the very essence of life. It tells me everything that has ever happened to the tree in other seasons—the sap beginning to soften and seep; the roots stretching out through the soil for food; the swelling of buds and the burst of young leaves; the angular shape of the tree made big and round as the leaves grew full and shaded the ground; the coolness given to children who threw themselves down under its canopy after playing themselves into exhaustion, their knees wishboned high and their chests heaving up and down as they laughed out the air they gasped in all at one time; the coming and going busyness of birds and squirrels seeking shelter for a time of new life; and the exquisite autumn farewell to the fullness and the leaves and the playing children and the wildlife, except for the few curmudgeons who would not give in to the cold.

What I see in the sturdy old trunks has been there all along. It was a part of everything that happened before but was covered up by other goings-on. It is God-created life, and *beautiful* is not a large enough word to describe it. *Good* is more fitting.

If I were old, I would hope that the sight of me would not sadden you. Or that you would not think of me as having lost so much that I once had. That isn't what happens with age. I will not have lost anything. I will have experienced and grown through everything that has happened to me. And although you won't be able to see my earlier times, they will nevertheless be mine. Because life is still mine—now, as it was when it began, and as it shall continue to be after I am gone. From your distance, you may not call it beautiful. But I, being closer to it, call it good.

If I were old—

Correction: *When* I am old . . .

# 8

## Good-bye Is an Angry Word

IT IS VERY HARD to love someone we are about to lose to death. Don't blame the Twelve for running out on Christ—we do it all the time to each other.

I remember when I was in the third grade and a new boy joined our class. His name was Stewart, a nice boy, sweet-natured and easy to like. But pale, and unusually clumsy. A few of the more athletic boys used to tease him now and then because he fell down a lot, but generally we all felt very friendly toward him. Then one day when Stewart was absent, which he frequently was, our teacher asked us to pray for him. And by all means not to tease him anymore. Stewart, she told us, was not going to live much longer, and she hoped that we would try to make his remaining days as happy as we could.

The announcement was a terrible shock for all of us. I had buried dead birds. I knew about the death of distant relatives. A good friend's mother had died, but that was before I knew her. Somehow death was like the weather in another part of the world; you knew about it, yet you didn't feel it. Stewart was making me feel it—and I was angry with him. I wanted to make him stop what he was doing, which was dying. And I couldn't. And I didn't

128

know what to do about it. I stopped talking to Stewart. I avoided him at recess. Then one day as we were lining up outside school after lunch, Stewart stepped on my foot, which wasn't unusual for him to do, and I hit him. I hit him very hard on the back with my fist because I had to hit somebody and I couldn't very well hit God, although He was the one I really was angry with.

Stewart had a board strapped to his back under his thin cotton shirt. Some of the other children had whispered about it, but now I actually felt it. My hand stung from the impact against it and I started to cry. Not because my hand hurt, but because I had done harm to Stewart when all I really wanted to do was love him. But he was hard to love, because I was so angry. Not at him, but at God for allowing such a thing as death. Nevertheless Stewart was the one I had hurt. I made him cry. He forgave me, but it took a long time for me to forgive myself.

I watched Stewart die from the sidewalk outside his house where I used to stand every day after school when Stewart was no longer strong enough to come to class. He used to sit in the dining-room window and wave to me. Sometimes his mother asked me in, but I never stayed long. I was afraid. Afraid to be where death might be. Afraid God might find out I was mad at Him. But I liked Stewart's mother. She was so soft-spoken, cheerful actually, and even though her eyes were red-circled, she never let me see her cry. Stewart had limp, sandy-colored hair that was always falling onto his forehead, and his mother used to reach out now and then and brush back the strands. When Stewart would pull away from her, as boys will do when their mothers are affectionate, she would give him a quick kiss on the back of his head and find something that needed doing in another room.

The morning after Stewart died, our teacher announced it at the beginning of class. Nothing else went well the rest of the day. Not for any of us. Even the best-behaved students got out of line, and the teacher had no patience with any of us. We were brutal at recess and lunchtime, using any excuse to pummel one another, until the principal had to come out to restore order. The rest of the day we sulked. We weren't normal again until the day of Stewart's funeral, which we didn't attend, but we knew what time it was, and something came over us after that. A certain letting go, I suppose you could call it. God had Stewart. The struggle was over.

I didn't realize it at the time, but Stewart's death was teaching me something I would only begin to understand much later: that love and death are never easy companions. And I have seen it happen not only again in my own life but in the lives of many others, this business of misdirected anger in the face of a loved one's impending death. We don't mean to do it, but instead of having it out with God, we turn our wrath upon the one we love. Some very loving families have been torn apart by the death of a child or a parent, not because they didn't have enough love but because their love was overwhelmed by their unspent anger at God. As Christians we are especially vulnerable to such confusion because we know that death is not an end to life and we think we should be able to take it in stride.

If anyone can share our fury, if anyone can agree with us that death is an unbearable outrage, it is God. He has never accepted death, and neither should we. Love is the very opposite of death, and it is fitting that they are mortal enemies. Christ Himself couldn't accept death, and at one point used His divine power to push death aside as He walked into a tomb and brought a cherished friend out of it, alive. Such power is beyond our capacity, but Christ's impulse certainly was human. Given the ability, wouldn't any of us do the same for a Lazarus in our life? Christ didn't accept His own death with ease. Being human enough to love life, He struggled with His Father to let Him go on living it here—never mind what goes on after death. Life here was what Christ was experiencing, and for all the tribulations in it, He found it sweet. He sweat blood trying to hold onto it, and only an intense feeling of oneness with God and with God's own anger against death enabled Him to do battle with their common enemy.

We aren't meant to take death in stride. Nor does our belief in a life after death make it any less painful to lose a loved one here in this life, the only one we have yet known. Death *is* an outrage, and we will find God agreeing with us if only we will carry our anger to Him instead of flinging it helplessly on the person we are going to lose.

This is a time for a special kind of love, one that is gentle with the dying and ferocious with death. It can only grow out of the ashes of anger that has burned openly in the sight of God.

Everyone knew it was going to happen. I received the news early because those who know me know I'm up early. Jessie made the call herself. Her mother had died.

"It's a blessing!" I thought, but didn't say it aloud. One doesn't. Yet it's a common reaction when someone has died after a long illness. For a long time we have watched what happens to those who stand by the bedside of a loved one who is dying. We have seen how deeply the pain is etched on the faces of those who know there is no hope, no cure. The waiting seems endless, and then finally it is over, and we pronounce it a blessing.

*We* call it that. And *we* are wrong. Because we don't really understand what is going on.

A death, any death, is not a blessing. It is the echo of a war that took place a long time ago. It was fought over our living bodies, and we are still deeply involved in the aftermath. Death was defeated, but did not die; it is still hovering in the shadows of our lives. It has lost its power to claim us, but it can still do us harm.

I saw what it did to Jessie.

Fifteen years ago her mother had a serious heart attack. It came out of nowhere. She survived, but her life was severely limited: Moderate exercise and as little stress as possible, plus a lot of medication. One more attack, it was said, would kill her.

Jessie was the youngest of three children. Her father was dead. Her older sister and brother were married and had children. Jessie had no serious plans at the time. She wasn't in love, she wasn't committed to her job, although she enjoyed it, and she liked living at home. Her mother was her best friend. It seemed only logical for Jessie to bear the burden of her mother's confinement—which she did for all those years.

She also managed to have a life of her own. She kept her job; she had good friends. When she could get someone to fill in for her at home, she went off on vacation, never very far. She even fell in love and considered getting married; but she never did. I didn't ask her why, and she didn't tell me. But I could guess. So could everyone. Caring for her mother made it impossible for Jessie to meet the demands of a husband and children; she was wise enough to understand that from the beginning.

Jessie was not an unhappy person. In fact, she was one of the most thoughtful, cheerful, sympathetic women I have ever known. If you had reason to celebrate, Jessie was right there to congratulate you; if you needed to cry, she could sense it and she'd stay until the tears were gone. I used to wonder how she could go on giving so much love when she wasn't getting much back.

Her mother tried to be self-sufficient, but she was so afraid of her own fragility that she avoided leaving the house. For a while she welcomed visitors, but even that proved to be too much of a strain, and she spent most of her time alone, waiting for Jessie to come home from work. A new problem was beginning: Jessie's mother was becoming seriously depressed, which not only made her difficult to live with but threatened her physical condition. She ate so little that she was becoming weak. Occasionally she was hospitalized for several weeks.

But that wasn't the worst of it.

Jessie's mother knew she would never recover, and the imminence of death assaulted her personality. She had been a lot like Jessie—concerned and caring—but gradually she became demanding, resentful, accusing. Jessie could never do enough to please her, and more than once I saw her fight back tears under the sting of her mother's verbal attacks. And then her mother would cry and hold out her bone-thin arms to Jessie, and the two of them would hold onto each other for dear life. Jessie never, at least in my presence, spoke sharply in return. She kept her tears out of sight. Her affection was genuine.

Finally Jessie's mother remained in the hospital, and it was obvious that she would never come home again. Jessie took time off from work to sit by her bedside for hours every day. She read the newspaper to her mother and thought of funny little bits of gossip to tell her. Her mother slipped in and out of consciousness toward the end, but

Jessie kept reading and talking—just in case, she said. Maybe her mother could hear more than the doctors realized, and the sound of her daughter's voice would tell her she was not alone.

When her mother died, Jessie herself was very ill. She hadn't been eating well, she needed sleep, and her emotions were rubbed raw. We prayed she would be all right in time. And in time she was.

But she was not the same.

Still thoughtful, still kind, right there to cheer you when you needed it—but a little sad underneath it all. You could tell that the sadness would never go away. It was a wound inflicted during a fierce battle Jessie had fought. With death.

And she had won.

It was a battle many of us will be called to fight. Because if we love someone who is going to die, then we are the ones death will be out to get. Not to kill us, because death doesn't have that power anymore. It's our love that death is after, and he is quite capable of destroying it.

## How Can I Deal with Death?

Now I have to come to terms with Jesus Christ. With who He is and what He did—to me and for me—and why.

I always thought I knew what He meant. But that was when I was younger and thought I knew what everything meant. I had no problem believing that I was going to live forever, because I was so full of life, it simply had to last as far as the mind could see. And, of course, life to me meant life as I knew it: here, now, in this human form. Something in me kept trying to tell me that I didn't have it straight, but it couldn't get through. I wanted no part of nay-sayers. I loved life and I wasn't going to give it up.

I love life even more now that I have known it longer. But my mind cannot see as far in front of me as it did in my earlier years.

I believe that I will live forever. But I know now that the life I live beyond the one I have already tasted is going to be different. And I find it hard to hold onto what I cannot see.

Yet I also find it very hard to grasp a lot of things here in this world—because I don't know enough about them, either. Medical technology, for instance. It's far beyond me, and I'm not sure how I feel about such things as transplants and machines that can keep us alive after our own bodies have ceased to function properly. I believe in using the intelligence God gave us, but I am horrified when we poison our world as we make it more efficient. I don't know if the pain we cause and the loss we endure as we try to lengthen our life are right or wrong, good or bad.

I don't think I will ever know, at least not while I am here. I don't think I will ever know what my life will be like when I am not here—*while* I am here.

And I feel I should apologize to God, and most certainly to His Son, because I try to know. I'm afraid that God may not like my wanting to know. He may expect my faith to be certain.

No. Not at all. I'm forgetting that God is not an outsider. Nor a vapor. If I want to know who He is and how He feels about life, I can get an inkling by understanding myself and my own feelings. I am at least a little like God. By design. And He is, in a few ways, a little like me. In my times of wondering it is important for me to remember this resemblance, this relatedness. It is a means of communication between God and me at a critical time.

My doubts, my questions, my wonderings are part of my being human. God knows it. He knows the reason for it, too. I have always been afraid of death, and I still am.

I am not wayward in God's eyes. Or unusual. He has had to assure me in many other forms. He remembers me as a man of influence whose daughter lay near death, a man who came to Christ for a miracle because Christ could deal with death and a man can't. God knows me as a relative of a man stricken with a crippling disease; He has heard my groans as I helped to lower the man down through an opening in a roof so that he could be brought to Christ's attention ahead of all the other seekers in that congregation.

Seekers—of what?

An escape from death.

Some of them didn't say as much. They spoke of other needs: sight, sanity, the ability to walk and run again, an end to disfigurement and deterioration. But what they were really saying was: *"Save me from death!"* Some of them asked for those they loved to be saved, but they knew that eventually they too would need saving.

Like me, they couldn't believe what they knew to be true: that He could bring the dead to life. But like me, they could believe *Him*. Some had seen proof, some hadn't; it made no difference. The presence of God can be felt.

So, then, there is a precedent. Others have asked this monumental favor of God. Can't I? Can't I ask, on behalf of one I love, to have death put off? And don't I know that I am asking for myself as well, because someday I will be at this brink? I may not see it coming, as I do in the life of my ill friend. Death may come for me suddenly, from behind, without time for this urgent question. *Lord, will You save me from death? You promised!*

And how well I know in my better moments that He has already done it. He has gone beyond where He was when

He was here among us as a Man. Oh, He raised many from the dead then, because that was the only way He could hold onto them. He could give them a little more time, much as we can do now with our scientific miracles. And that was important—that delay, that barter with time— because there was something lasting He had to do.

He defeated death. He did all the dying that had to be done, and with His agony He bought us life.

I wonder, though, will that assurance sustain me if *I* am the one who must face the slow approach of death? Will it enable *me* to go on loving those who must watch me leave? Can I say good-bye without blaming them for letting me go? Without resenting them for remaining here in this familiar place? I would not want to leave them devastated by the blows of my bitterness.

But what will I do with my rage against the unchangeable realization that part of me is mortal and must end?

I hope that I will vent it completely—and in the form of love. Because love is not a subjugation of our human feeling, but rather the most forceful way we can express them. It is Christ daring to care about a mother's grief, a friend's sense of abandonment, a wrongdoer's terror of the penalty—and *doing* something about them from His imprisonment on a cross. I can think of no better way to humiliate death. And no more eloquent way to let death know that I am more than mortal.

My great-grandmother, even though she couldn't speak, died with love in her eyes for all of us—and all of us were there. A friend's father, painfully afflicted, found words to make his fellow patients laugh. A woman of great dignity shook her fist at death when she asked her family to sing for her as they gathered around her bed in her final moments here.

It is possible for us to love that hard. And with that much rage.

## Can I Afford to Love This Much?

Don't ever forget that death was defeated, but not destroyed. We still use the word *dying* to describe what happens when someone we love leaves this human experience. It's all we know. We see death in the room and we turn away, remembering the power he once had over us. We don't dare to stare him down. And rightly so. We can't. That is God's battle.

We have another battle to fight. Can we save our love from death, as God Himself saved us? Can we allow ourselves to suffer?

Suffering is giving more than your love. You give part of your life—in the sense that nothing and no one else is as important as the needs of the one you love. It's knowing that you will go through the rest of your life with a little something lost, because you will never get back what you have given. It belongs to the person you love and it will go with that person. So you had better be sure you can afford to give your way of life, your time, your patience, your injured feelings, your exhaustion, your many hopes and disappointments. And you had better be sure you aren't, in some hidden corner of your being, thinking that in some way God will compensate you for your loss. He won't. He's given. He knows better.

Suffering is accepting pain you could otherwise avoid. It's looking into the eyes of someone who knows that this part of life is ending. It's taking the blows of that person's fear of what's to come. It's honoring impossible hopes and sudden, unaccountable improvements that may not last. It's sharing the ordeal, knowing you can't make it end but you can make it bearable.

Suffering celebrates life in the very face of death—holding onto the one you love until you feel God's hand taking the place of yours. It is demonstrating the power of love, which is life, over the power of fear, which is death. It is putting yourself between the one you love and the grisly curious stare of death.

Death will not take your suffering kindly. It will put you to the most grueling test of your life.

It will contort, before your eyes, the face of the one you love. It will waste a body that was once strong and vital. It will cloud a mind that was once clear. It will fling the dust of misunderstanding in your face and gloat over your reaction of hurt and indignation. It will scatter old injuries like marbles under your feet as you approach the one you love. It will raise your voices and fill your mouths with exaggerations.

Worse than that, death will see to it that your suffering is not admired. You will be called a fool. When you ask for water, you'll be given something sour-tasting. You may feel a spear in your side.

But if you can endure these abuses, you will save your love from death. You will defeat fear. And you will be able to look at the person you love and see not the mask that death has painted, but the exquisite being God has not ceased creating.

# 9

---

## You Look the Same to Me

---

WE WERE JUST FINISHING our coffee and—yes, older women do it too—we started talking about men. Husbands, generally, and then specifically. We are three fairly self-sufficient women, so we don't want to fall into the trap of picking on men for all that's wrong with the world. We know better. And we don't think of men as little boys, either, so the conversation wasn't on that plane. We were talking about men as human beings, as friends, and as partners.

"When I married Steve, I thought he was the smartest, the strongest, and the most sensitive man I had ever known," my friend Fran said. "That was a long time ago— and I feel the same way about him now."

I was surprised. Happily so, because many women don't put enough value on those qualities in a man. But Fran's husband had lost his job six months earlier, and that puts a strain on any marriage relationship. Steve worked for a large paper company that went out of business. He had a lot of experience, he was good at his job, which was selling, but he was in his early fifties, and it isn't easy for a man to get a job at that age. Fortunately Fran was a nurse, so they had an income. But they also had four children in various stages of being educated. They counted every penny. Always did. Now it was a matter of how many pennies could be brought in.

I hadn't seen Fran or Steve for a long time, which I didn't think was odd. When hard times hit, who feels like having friends over for dinner? I kept track of them through other friends, who told me that Steve went into business for himself. He was a paper broker, using his years of know-how to bring manufacturers and customers together. Maybe it would work. We all hoped it would. But even if it did, Steve and Fran would have other problems. We all knew what happens to a man when he loses his job—and to the woman who may lose her ability to love him.

It's very hard to live with defeat, and that's really what hard times are. They mean we were beaten. Never mind what the reasons were, they don't count. We lost. That counts. We did our best, or so we like to think, but it wasn't good enough. Or maybe we weren't good enough. Maybe we never will be. You don't have to be a man to understand that; women know it, too. But defeat is rougher on men because they're expected to be winners.

We don't really know how the followers of Christ were received back home after they were defeated. I don't imagine they were easy to live with, and probably they were impossible to love. They had built their lives around a Man who was executed, and in an atmosphere of ridicule. The dreams, the hopes, were gone. Maybe a man could go back to making nets or tents, maybe he could get work on a fishing boat if the owner didn't know who he was. But the chances were slim. And besides, those men had gone into another field of work. They had become disciples, and they were good at it. But their jobs were gone because their Leader was gone, and very likely they didn't know who they were anymore. They had lost their identity along with the job, which is something that often happens to men.

Defeat has a way of making us unlovable. It shouts in our ear that the best parts of ourselves are shabby, below par, inadequate. And we find it hard to argue with that accusation, because we have, indeed, been rejected. So we turn on ourselves, despising what is best in us and giving full rein to what is worst. It's hard for anyone to love us, distorted as we are, and a woman who tries to love a defeated man has her work cut out for her. She will not succeed if she loses her own identity.

When our own identity is so much a part of another person's, then that person's defeat becomes ours as well. The way we love changes as the person we are trying to love changes. We begin to love softly, because we're afraid to hurt someone who has already been hurt. We touch too gingerly, because we don't want to appear pushy. We tiptoe through the other person's fears and self-accusations—as if we agree with them. And very often we do. Eventually. Because we begin to attack our own judgment and ask ourselves how we could ever have loved the person whose life we are trying to share right now. Look—how can anyone deny it? He's not the same as he was!

Neither are we. We're not very lovable, either.

It's possible that we would never have heard anything more about a group of defeated disciples if their resurrected Leader hadn't gone looking for them. And by that time they had lost so much of themselves that they didn't recognize Him when He stood among them. He had to *identify* Himself. More than once. Then He had to remind them who they still were. Only then could they embrace. Only then could they begin to push defeat back.

There may be something here for those of us who are

going through hard times. It may be that the only way for a woman to go on loving a defeated man is to remember who he really is and to be who she is. She may be able to remind both of them of their identities if she can say, "When I married you, I thought you were the smartest, the strongest, and the most sensitive man I ever knew, and those things were important to me. They still are, and I still feel the same way about you."

I think this is what my friend Fran was talking about.

## Who Are You?

On the train one morning I sat behind two men who were talking about a friend who had lost his job. Both men had gone through a similar experience and they were sympathetic.

"It's the worst time I ever had," one said.

"Don't remind me," the other said. "I felt so ashamed."

"I know. I'd sit outside some guy's office waiting for an interview, trying to look confident—and I felt like a bum."

"You, too?"

"Sure. How else can you feel? Nobody wants you."

A young woman fresh out of college went through it, too. She was a marketing major looking for a job with a large corporation, and she was very nervous about her first interview. "I bought a navy blue suit," she told me. "I hope it's all right. I want to give the right impression."

She didn't. Nor did she get the job. "Everything was going pretty well until they asked me to describe myself—in three words. So I thought a minute and said, 'Ambitious, hardworking, and anxious.' "

I admired her accuracy—and her honesty. "I would have hired you," I said.

"Well, they didn't. They wanted something like 'loyal, cheerful, and dependable.' "

"But you're those, too!" I protested.

"*Too* wasn't enough," she said. "That was *all* they wanted."

Her confidence was shaken. "It hurts to get rejected," she said.

Rejection does more than hurt. It shatters our image of ourselves. It calls into question everything we believed or tried to be or hoped to accomplish. In the coldest of terms it asks us, What on earth are we doing here?

Rejection is being told, "We don't need you," by someone who may not even know you. It's being asked for certain credentials you don't have.

Sorry. Next, please!

So you begin to ask yourself, Who am I?—because *if* you're somebody, then you ought to be able to prove it. May we see your driver's license and at least one major credit card?

Rejection marks the difference between being accepted and being loved. Acceptance takes what it needs from us; love takes all there is. Acceptance asks for our credentials; love knows who we are.

Some years ago I had to start my life over again. My marriage ended, unexpectedly, the house where I had lived was sold, and I was working on a book that would take a long time to complete. I needed a place to live, and I was going to need some sort of income to sustain me until my book was finished. I felt pretty desperate, but I was able to keep panic at bay by telling myself that I would just have to solve one problem at a time.

Then I encountered my greatest problem, which was one I hadn't even anticipated: The world didn't want any part of me. The world couldn't even acknowledge my existence, because I didn't have any credentials. There was no record of credit cards or bank accounts in my name only; I had held salaried jobs, but not for some time; I was a self-employed writer, which apparently was the same thing as having no visible means of support. I was not exactly young. I had a driver's license, but didn't own a car.

I was denied credit; I had difficulty opening my own bank accounts; and I had to put up quite a fight to get a one-year lease on a house I wanted to rent.

At the time I called it discrimination, but I know now that it wasn't. A man in my situation would have had just as much trouble. The world didn't know who I was—because it has difficulty acknowledging the existence of people who are alone. It doesn't know how to classify us.

I had earned my living all my adult life. I had been responsible to family and friends. I had given and received a great deal of love. But none of my credentials revealed these facets of my being. My records showed only that I had been attached to other persons at various points in my life—and suddenly I was no longer attached. It was like applying for a job and being asked to describe myself in three words that no one wanted to hear: I was alone. And the world, not knowing what else to do with me, denied me credentials. Admission. Approval. Perhaps my situation was only temporary—Could I come back in a year and reapply? By then I might be attached again, to something or someone that could verify my existence. No. I didn't think my situation was going to change, at least not in that manner.

Sorry. Next, please!

Now, several years later, I have a handful of credit cards in my name; they also bear all kinds of numbers and letters to assure the world that I am here. The tellers at my bank call me by name. The owner of my house has become a friend who thinks a lease is just a silly formality that I insist on signing. My mailbox is stuffed with solicitations, invitations, and brochures from people and organizations I never heard of. Finally the world proclaims it knows me.

But it doesn't. And it never will.

My credentials say nothing about me. They record some of my habits and preferences. They indicate how much of my income I am willing to spend, and in what manner. They will tell you what the world finds acceptable about me—but they do not identify me. They will not tell you that I mean what I say. Or that I care about your hard times. Or that I enjoy meeting people and learning something about them. Or that I worry about people without homes—and worry even more about the way I might feel if they slept on my doorstep. My credentials won't give you a clue to my self-doubts, to my impatience with incompetence, to my occasional rage at indifference, or to my feelings of hurt when I am misunderstood.

My driver's license, my educational degree, and my record of employment will tell you some of the things I can do. But not what I can't do and wish I could. Or what I have tried to do and failed at—and how I feel about my failures.

My credentials, now that I have them, won't give you any clue to my identity. They will only tell you what the world wants of me—and that is such a small part of myself. If you want to learn my identity, then you will have to love me and allow me to love you. And, as you know, that is not a simple matter.

When we go through hard times, we lose our credentials. But we can deal with that; we can get them back. We can get another job, however long it takes. We can start over, more than once. Yes, we do have to make our way in this world. No one can deny that. We do have to feed, clothe, and shelter ourselves and those we love. But what happens to us as we are doing all these things is more important. We can survive the humiliations, the anxieties, the disappointments, the fears, defeat itself—if we know who we are.

## Who Needs You?

When I was without credentials, I lost what was left of my self-confidence. I would have been grateful to curl up in the corner of a small room where I was in no one's way. I would have lived on what little money I had for as long as I could—and then, who knows? I couldn't even consider the word *try*; trying takes strength, and I had none. For the only time in my life I was grateful that I didn't have children to look after.

But I did have an elderly dog and a young cat. And I loved them very much. God made good use of that love.

Obviously I couldn't live in a corner of a room. I needed not only a house but some land around it, not for me but for my animals. I couldn't curl up somewhere and eat as little as possible; I had to exercise my animals and feed them decently. I had to pay for medical care if they needed it. I had to give attention to their needs, one of which was to play and have fun.

I had to go on living. And loving. And I didn't think I could. I thought God was unfair to make such demands on me, and I asked to be excused from my responsibilities. He turned me down. I was another disciple on a misty shore pleading with Christ to have mercy on my weakness. Consider my defects, I begged. What would You want with someone like me?

He wanted a great deal.

And then He showed me His hands and His side, and

He reminded me that I had said I would never let Him down. When I tried to explain that I was a failure, He wouldn't allow me to finish. He knew all about that, He said. He was the most obvious failure the world had ever seen.

Credentials?

There were myths and rumors about His birth, but who could believe them? Occupation? A carpenter, apparently, but not known for any outstanding piece of work. Who were His last three customer? Did He carry references? Some people claimed He was a king. Nonsense! Look at Him—the way He dresses, the people who crowd around Him. A revolutionary? Not according to the things He says. A philosopher? A priest, perhaps? The temple authorities would never agree.

Oh, well, it doesn't matter now, does it? He's gone. Died like a common criminal.

Such a Man refused to pity me. He would not excuse me from the struggles in life. He saw what God valued in me, even if the world didn't. He called me by my proper name, which made me realize that defeat had taken my credentials but not my identity. All I had left in the world was my love for a gentlemanly dog and a rascally cat, and I couldn't let go of it. That one characteristic was something I recognized as an authentic part of myself; it had survived rejection. Perhaps more of me remained? My ability to concentrate on what I had to do, my willingness to take a risk, my patience with chaos and my determination to make order out of it, my joy in my friends, the challenge I found in my work—if I searched very hard, I might find some remnants of the qualities God had given me a long time ago. Better yet, if Christ could point them out to me . . . somehow I knew I could count on Him to do that.

I did not gain strength. I still yearned for a dark corner somewhere—but I didn't have time to look for one. I did not have hope—that is, if you define hope as some fluttering, leaping, energizing sensation. I had a telephone that enabled me to make inquiries about houses for rent. I had two feet and a rented car to take me to see them. And when I say I fought to obtain a lease on a house that was perfect for my needs, don't think I fought vigorously. I couldn't. All I had was persistence, but it was enough. I also remembered professional acquaintances who needed the kind of work I could do, but in small amounts, which was exactly what I required.

Nothing happened overnight. It took months and, in some cases, years to rebuild my life. But it began and it was accomplished with the help of a resurrection kind of love—which is the only way I can describe what it takes to love someone who is going through hard times. And by resurrection, I mean a love that can see through the lies defeat tells about us.

## Whose Side Are You On?

When someone you love is going through hard times, what do you do?

You love him—naturally.

You pitch right in and get a job if he loses his. Or maybe you get a second job if you already have one. There's no end to your strength. You do whatever needs to be done. He can lean on you for as long as he must.

You find ways to keep him busy. He can help around the house. He can do the shopping. He makes a lot of mistakes, but you correct him; you never criticize him.

When your friends ask about him, you say he's fine and change the subject. You know he'd be ashamed if anyone knew he was depressed. You tell the children to be considerate.

You praise him every chance you get. You tell him he's wonderful. When he's going for an interview, you're sure he'll get the job. If he doesn't—well, he was overqualified.

You feel so sorry for him. You know how much it must hurt.

You mean well. I believe it. But you're not on his side. You're behaving as if the person you love is not a person you need—and the world has already told him that.

And what about you? How do you feel?

Aren't you afraid? Worried? And perhaps just a little bit contemptuous because here you are doing so much and he's not doing anything? Oh, yes, he's trying. But he's not succeeding. Maybe he *doesn't* have what it takes. Maybe he *is* out of date and too old to change.

You're looking at him through the world's eyes. No wonder you don't like what you see.

## Don't Accept Any Counterfeits

Don't mistake a change in a situation for a change in the person. The man who lost his job is still the person you were able to love when he had a job. He may help around the house, but he has to do it in his own way. Teach him if he doesn't know how, but don't impose your way on him. If you don't like the results, criticize. Don't correct. He can do that for himself.

If you're worried, say so. He can handle it even if he thinks he can't.

If you're afraid, admit it. Both you and he will find some relief in knowing you're not alone.

He doesn't deserve your pity, but he does need your compassion. Pity speaks from a distance; compassion gets close enough to cry. So if you feel tears coming on, don't hold them back. Let him know you feel his hurt.

Hold onto your own identity. You don't have to be a heroine; it doesn't suit you. You still have needs and you can't meet all of them. Don't stop offering them, along with the rest of what you are, to the person you love. Because if you try to stop needing him, then you're rejecting him.

A resurrection kind of love will not accept what defeat says about a person. It knows the truth. If the person you love behaves like someone else, call him by his proper name. Refuse to deal with anyone less. If there is confusion about his identity, you can end it.

Shame huddles in the dark places. Don't go there. Call the person you love out into the light. When friends ask, "How is he?"—tell them. Put them in touch with him. Don't hide defeat from your children; let them discover how to confront it. Admit how difficult life is right now. Let your struggle show.

In other words, be the person he can recognize. And love. Because he needs to love. Especially now. Loving will tell him who he is. That's the only credential he—and you—will ever need. It's the only one you can't afford to lose.

# 10

## Love Goes by the Rules

DON'T.

Don't expect your life, or your love, to be the same as it was. Ever.

Don't ask to be compensated—by anyone—for being hurt.

Don't wait for time to heal the hurt. You need more than time.

If you are looking for a way to go on loving someone who was unfaithful, then you need all the help God can give you. And, believe me, He does understand what you're going through. After all, He still loves us.

You may think you know what's ahead for you in this attempt to restore love. You may even see a few advantages in the remorse of the one who hurt you. Suddenly, amid the angry words, the threats and tears on both sides, your relationship has become more intense. Once more, after years of quiet trust, you and the one you love are the most important, most consuming interests of your lives. It can be heady stuff. You may think your love is young again. And exciting. And anxious. And so promising.

It is none of these things.

Your love has become suspicious, afraid that what hap-

pened will happen again. Your love is afraid to trust, yet
wants to with all its heart—and feels guilty when it can't. It
is angry, not only because it was hurt, but for *allowing* itself
to be hurt. How could your love be so blind? It has lost faith
in its judgment and can't believe what it sees. It wonders,
too, if the one who was hurt might have been at fault.
Somehow. And so your love is very cautious. It has no protection.

We are not born loving. We are born wanting. And the
two are not the same. We want what satisfies us, and the
satisfaction, once completed, may end the wanting. Which
is fine for many, many of our needs. My hunger tells me
that I need food to supply energy for my life, so I eat. I'm
tired at the end of the day, so I sleep. If I've been too long
alone, then I *want* to be with people, but several good times
with good friends make me *want* to be alone. Going to the
ballet satisfies my need for a close-up, live creative experience; it makes me want to write as well as the dancers leap.
I say that I love all these things that I need and do—but I
don't. Not really. I want them.

If I want someone in my life, it's because that person
makes me feel better about myself. He fills my need to laugh,
to talk, to go places in his company, to be affectionate, or to tell
him how I feel at a particular moment about a particular event
or a particular person. I may want him to respond to my
intelligence, if he thinks I have it, or to my sense of humor, if
he can enjoy it, or to mingle with my gloom, and I do have
those times. There's nothing wrong with wanting such things
or wanting someone to be a part of them. But they have
nothing to do with love. I can want someone deeply, desperately, devotedly—and not love him at all.

Love is concerned with the needs of another. Not only
with some of another's needs, but with all of them, includ-

ing those that are not wanted. Love is an investment of myself into the building of another person. It is not a prize for being the best or the most desired at the moment. It is not a reward for making me feel good about myself. It is my appreciation of who a person is and my interest in who that person will become. Obviously love is not an investment I can afford to make casually.

Love needs rules. We can't just love each other and be the same persons we were before it happened. Loving each other means living in different ways. We have to allow ourselves to be changed by love. I can say I love you and still lie to you; I can tell myself that I don't want the truth to hurt you, when in reality the truth will draw my own blood. But if I am ruled by my love for you, then I will be crucified upside down rather than lie to you. That calls for a lot of courage, I know, but love is supposed to make me a better person, not a more clever one.

This matter of rules has always been a source of conflict between God and us, and among ourselves. From the beginning of time God has been handing down rules to us, and we kept breaking them, insisting that no human being could live by them. And finally Jesus Christ had to show us that the rules *were* love, and that if we don't follow the rules, then we aren't loving. Just as the Word had to become flesh, the feeling of love has to become the acts of love.

It *is* possible for us to love beyond the damage of an infidelity. Not wildly or spontaneously, perhaps. Not by a list of dos and don'ts and a sharp eye out for the first violation. Not as an atonement for a wrong done, or as an overbearing pretense that it never happened. That only twists the dagger in the wound. And the wound needs healing—but by an awareness that both persons have suffered deeply and by a willingness to feel each other's pain. By realizing that love isn't something we make up as we go along. Love has been around longer than we have, and it isn't trendy. It goes by the rules, and they aren't easy to follow.

For starters, if I love you, then I must put you before me. In everything. It's what Christ called giving up my life for you. Not *to* you, but *for* you. And I don't give up my life to love as *I* interpret love, but as God does. He lets me know what I must and must not do *if* I love you. Not that I'll always like what I must do. That isn't the point. The point is, *if* I love you, then what love wants is more important than what I want. Neither one of us tells the other how to live. Love does. Those are the rules. And they apply to both of us, particularly if we are starting all over again to learn how to love each other.

## Believe It—Love Isn't There Anymore

It happens to other people. You read about it in books. But it doesn't really happen. Not to you.

Every night when you go to bed you tell yourself it isn't real. But when you wake in the morning with tears in your eyes, it has to be real. The person you love doesn't love you—anymore. He loves someone else instead.

Then where does that leave you?

You didn't intend to love for a little while. You meant it. Forever. That's what love is to you: forever. It doesn't change its mind. It doesn't see someone or something it likes better than you. It keeps on loving. Forever.

Then why are you waking up with tears in your eyes?

And why are you asking yourself what you could have done, or not done, to keep someone loving—forever? Why are you searching your mind for a way to bring love back?

And why are you asking God how He could allow this to happen?

These are questions that have already been answered. The problem is that you don't want to face the answers.

You must.

It *is* over, this love that was supposed to last for all time.

Perhaps you could have done something to delay it, or prevent it. Perhaps you were at fault, at least a little. But perhaps the person you loved deserves some of the blame, too. Perhaps time was to blame. Or the fact that you had different interests. The children? What did they have to do with it? Did you give them too much of your attention?

Stop.

You could go on forever. You could blame the world, the way things are, your own development or the lack of it; fatigue could have done it, or money worries. How about the pressures of work and getting ahead? Where you live? All those problems in blurbs on the covers of magazines you don't have time to read? Sex—too much on your mind or possibly not enough? Separate interests—or not enough that you share? Education—is one of you better educated than the other? How about night school? Is a parent living with you? Is he or she the culprit?

No. All these possibilities, or some of them, may have been present. But they didn't make it happen.

The person you loved stopped loving you. That is what happened. That is the cause, the problem, and the pain. Look no further.

Of course you want to. Because you think that if you can find a reason, you can change reality.

The reason doesn't matter. The reality does.

And reality keeps telling you that you are not lovable—anymore. You don't know which hurts more: losing the person you love or finding out that you aren't loved.

## Do Something

Did someone say, "I'm sorry"?

What shabby words they are. They're like Pilate, washing his hands and walking away from it all. They describe the offender's pain. They cry out for sympathy undeserved. They eradicate the fact that an offense was committed, that pain was inflicted. And the unfaithful person is no different for having uttered them. The offense can be committed again, and likely will be—unless there is a change in the person, in motivations, values, and sensitivities. Only love can do that—or, more accurately, our observance of the rules of love.

The same is true of the one who is offended. Only love and the basic change it makes in a person can effect forgiveness. Only love can bring a new relationship out of the ashes of one that has died. Only love can change "I'm sorry" to "I care."

"I care"—the words are fewer, simpler, but so much harder to come by.

"I care" means I share your pain. I am involved with your life. I *can't* walk away.

"I care" means I am being shaped by love—God's, Christ's, and my own.

The distance between "I'm sorry" and "I care" is not a pleasant journey, and you may not wish to take it. You, too, can walk away, you and your unlovableness. But you must do something. There is more than a relationship at stake.

What must be decided is: Will you, or will you not, love?

## What Will You Do with Your Anger?

Love? You don't even want to think about it. This is no time for patience and understanding. You can't be kind.

And you can't believe God expects it of you.

He doesn't. But He does expect you to be honest—with Him and with yourself.

Don't hide from God because you're angry. Don't misunderstand where He fits into your life. He doesn't want your company only when you can speak civilly. If your rage brings bitter words to your lips and hot tears to your eyes, He can hear them and taste them with you.

You are not behaving badly. You are not out of control. You are not overreacting. You are hurt. And God knows very well how that feels.

But—doesn't He expect you to pull yourself together? To handle this situation with some degree of poise? Not yet. You can't possibly. You don't even know, yet, what the situation is.

You only know that you're in pain, and that it keeps screaming inside you. And you wonder if you'll ever know peace again. You're grieving over the death of love. You're afraid; you know you're not a child, but if only someone would pick you up and hold you close.

Where does love fit into such a grim picture?

It *is* the picture. Everything you're feeling is your love crying out in protest.

Or did you think that love can only speak softly? Or that it is incapable of rage and vengeful desires? Have you never heard of the wrath of God?

It was love betrayed that drove us out of Eden. It turned its back on us and left us to encounter pain. It delivered us into captivity, led us into confusion, struck us down. Love betrayed denied an old man his dream of reaching a promised land; it wounded a cherished king through the deceit of his son; it shriveled up a tree that would not bear fruit.

God, too, knows such anger as yours. Let Him see it.

Let Him help you heal it. Don't deny love its right to cry
out. It is love's way of staying alive.

## Do You Want This Relationship?

Infidelity doesn't mean the end of a marriage. Do you
want yours to go on?

You don't see how it can, do you? You know you can't
*make* someone love you. And you can't *make* yourself love
someone who has hurt you so deeply.

But friends are telling you to be patient. What happened
isn't rare, they say. A lot of marriages have survived the
"other woman." Can yours?

Perhaps you hadn't thought about that possibility. You
were too preoccupied with the prospect of being abandoned. But maybe you aren't. You were so certain that love
was over. But maybe it isn't. Maybe the two of you can pick
up where you left off. After all, there is such a thing as
forgiveness.

Yes, there is. But it isn't a pronouncement you can
make. God will tell you that.

In a recent, much-publicized trial, a man was accused of
involvement in a plot to buy and sell drugs. As the case
went to the jury, the defendant told reporters, "It's all up
to God now"—as if he himself had nothing to do with what
might happen.

Nothing is ever *all* up to God, and certainly not in matters of forgiveness. He works with us, not instead of us. If
the offense is so large that we can't quite cover the distance
between where we are and where the offender is, then,
yes, we can ask Christ to make up the difference. But our
asking is crucial; it means we are reaching as far as we can.
It involves us in forgiveness.

When we call on Christ to embrace a loved one who has

hurt us, we are also asking Him to expand our own capacity to receive the pain a loved one has caused. We can't deny it, or any part of it, any longer. We have to surrender to it, as Christ did on the cross, before any healing can begin. We have to know the extent of the damage.

Can your marriage endure forgiveness? Can you?

There is an easier way out. The two of you can try to go on as you were—with a few changes, of course. You can be very cordial with each other, very polite, very distant, and very apprehensive. You'll watch him every minute, and he'll know you're watching. You won't believe a word he says about why he isn't where you expect him to be; you won't like the way he looks at other women, and you'll read incontrovertible proof of infidelity in the way other women look at him. Intimacy will be impossible; you'll have to work too hard to protect yourselves from each other. The slightest disagreement will threaten both of you, and you'll avoid discussing anything vital to either of you. Even your silences will be suspect: What are you *really* thinking?

Forgiveness is impossible in such an environment. Because love is gone. Resentment, hate, self-doubt have taken its place. The love you once had for each other, the love you insist you're resuming, is dead. You're resuming a conflict that has never been resolved.

## Considerate Love

Your marriage can survive an infidelity only if the two of you allow yourselves to experience love from scratch. Newly and honestly. This time you have to go by the rules. This time love has its eyes open; it considers what is real. You begin your relationship not as two wonderful people who think they know all there is to know about each other, but as two flawed human beings. You will be aware of some of your imperfections, but not all. They will lead you to some needs you didn't know you had. And now that you know this much about each other, you will realize that there is more to discover. You may even find areas of strength, understanding, and support you didn't know were there.

You won't pretend to be comfortable with each other. You won't accept approval in place of caring. You won't ask what cannot be given.

You will consider what has happened to each of you. Yes: to *each* of you.

You're well aware that you have been hurt. But so has he. Like you, he wonders if he is lovable. Or if he can really love. Each of you will have to consider how little you may love yourselves. And you will have to consider the fact that you can't make each other feel good about yourselves. Only God can do that.

You are not so far apart, you two. Each of you has been stung by the discovery that you are not what you thought you were. You never thought you could want someone to suffer. But you did. And you're not sure you're over it. He never thought he could deceive deliberately. He saw himself as well-meaning. And he isn't.

You're not exceptional. We all paint glowing images of ourselves, and if we happen to gain a sudden insight into the truth, we accept it like a photograph that doesn't do us justice. "That doesn't even look like me!" It's one of the reasons why some men and women didn't follow after Christ. They complained that He asked too much of them; they had worked too hard to get where they were and they weren't going to give it up to walk down a road with a Man who didn't know where His next meal was coming from. But that wasn't what He asked, or why they refused.

Seeing ourselves as we really are is one of the most diffi-

cult things we can try to do. Yet that is what Christ asked—
and still asks—of us all. It doesn't require courage—far from
it—but it gives us courage in the process. We may not like
what we are, but at least we're familiar with it. Change,
even if it goes by the name of improvement, is alien terri-
tory where we have never set foot.

A good look at himself enabled a conniving tax collector
to discover that he also had generosity; it led a woman of
the streets into a community of dignity; it grasped a run-
away disciple by the collar and sent him out into a hostile
world with a message of love. It also brought self-
destruction to a man who could not see beyond his own
traitorous act.

The sight of ourselves involves more than a fascination
with our shortcomings. We can see, if we look long enough
in the light Christ makes available to us, that we could be
better than we are. And that is when we have to make our
decisions. Will we or will we not give up the image we have
worked so hard to create? Will we or will we not allow God
to complete what He began in us?

The renewal of a marriage will bring both of you into the
same strong light, and you will see things you would rather
call by gentler names. But you will also consider new responses.

Don't expect everything to change if you are trying to
recover from your wounds. Each of you will do many
things you did before, but you will do them honestly; you
will be growing and you won't always please each other.
You will also behave in ways that are new to you. The light
may be blindingly harsh, but you will need it to see who
you are.

You will watch. And he will know you are watching. But
both of you will understand that you have no choice, and

that understanding will soften your combativeness. You have reason to be unsure of each other, and of yourselves. You haven't loved each other, or known each other, long enough to trust. That will come in time. For now, you have each other's compassion for your separate anxieties.

You will need each other's courage for the risks ahead. For telling each other how you feel and what is important to you. For daring to confront and disagree, because you know that is part of identifying yourselves.

Considerate love is an honesty that grows out of an attempt to forgive. It stands nose-to-nose with the reality of who we are. And it began a long time ago when God decided to try to love us again. As He can assure you, forgiveness takes a long time. It doesn't make everything right, and it's anything but easy. But—it's still going on.

## Can You Love?

You may not have a choice in the matter of your marriage. It may be over. Or your attempt to renew it may not succeed.

But you're beginning to see that there are others in your life: children, friends, family members, new acquaintances. They care; so do you.

Yet there is that haunting reminder of the person you lost. You can't love him. And you wonder if you must, somehow.

The answer is yes. But you know that, don't you? Because not being able to love him gets in your way. It asks you questions about yourself and you don't have the answers. You can't love him as you once did, but you want to find another way. Because just when you feel loving toward the whole world, just when you believe your hurt is healed, you remember the person you cannot love. At times you actually hate him—and you don't want to hate anybody. Not because you want to be a "nice" person, but because hatred frightens you. It insists that you don't love, and you believe that you do. But as long as you hate, then you cannot forgive. And unless you forgive, you can't love.

You may not hate the person. You may hate his definition of you. You may hate the power he has to declare you no longer lovable. You may hate the doubt he has aroused in you about whether you *ever* were lovable. Was he lying long ago when he said he loved you? Is he lying now?

You may never know. And you may never find out what changed the way he felt about you. It's not essential that you do. Because whatever happened, it had something to do with the other person's capacity to love. Not with yours. You only thought it did. You gave him the power to define you. You didn't know yourself then.

But you do now. At least you're beginning to allow God to define you. And as you let go of other definitions, you will stop being afraid of the labels other people apply to you. You'll realize that they just don't stick. As you lose your fear of another's power over you, you will also lose your hate.

If you are considering the possibility that you can love someone who doesn't love you, then forgiveness has begun. As for finding a way to love that person—that's the next thing you have to consider.

# 11

---

## Because We Care

---

I HAVE NO REGRETS for the times I have tried to love and failed. I have no bitterness toward those who would not let me love them—and such things do happen. I am grateful for the times when I could love and be loved. Yet I think I have gained something from my failures as well as my successes. We all do—but it takes time to come to that realization.

Some of the angriest moments of my life have been spent remembering the loving things I did for someone who didn't appreciate them. And, like other people with similar memories, I would vow never to be so generous with my love the next time around. Once I actually stuck to my vow—and it was a time of astonishing deprivation. I found I didn't know how to communicate with anyone—because if I didn't allow myself to care about a person, then there wasn't a reason for a relationship. Love, apparently, is the way we talk to each other, even if we don't speak clearly.

One day it finally occurred to me that being taken for granted, put upon, asked for, taken from, cried upon, taken out on, really weren't important. The fact that I cared enough to put myself in such vulnerable positions at such crucial times *was* important. To me as well as to others.

It may be that love is actually the end result of that breath of life God put into us in the beginning. Somewhere along our journey we got the idea that we ought to get something back from it, but I don't think that was God's original intent. Getting loved back is pleasurable and satisfying beyond description, but it does not make us more than we already are. Loving—our loving of others—does. Because we don't know what we have, or what we are, until we are called upon to offer ourselves up to another. And the call doesn't come from another; it comes from within ourselves. It's an understanding, often one we can't put into words, of what another person needs; sometimes the person with the need doesn't even recognize it. Yet we respond with a quality we may not know is ours. And suddenly there it is. Wonderful! If this quality is accepted with joy by the one we love, more than wonderful! But if not, it is still ours. We may have lost at loving, but we have gained in love itself. We have made an important discovery, one we can share with others for the rest of our lives.

As in all our other provings and discoveries, the realization of who we are and what God enables us to do will cost us pain sometimes, certainly an effort greater than we have ever made. It may cost us disappointment and the discomfort of being wrongly perceived. Yet others have reached for this goal—Christ was one of them—and it is time we did, too.

## We Don't Need a Reason

I was deeply comforted in a time of mourning by a woman I really didn't know well. We had met several times, always with many other people around us, and we liked each other, but we observed the formality of acquaintances—until one day when she invited me to have lunch with her. "Nothing fancy," she said, "just some bacon, lettuce, and tomato sandwiches. But it would be nice to see you."

She knew nothing about my loss, and I had no intention of discussing it. A lot of time had passed, and I was supposed to be over it. I wasn't; I only appeared to be. I'm a very private person who can maintain a placid expression during the worst of times; it's my way of protecting myself. So the invitation was exactly what I needed: a chance to spend some time with a pleasant, agreeable person who didn't know me well enough to ask questions.

The only question she asked me was how I liked my bacon done. And I don't even remember what else we talked about. But I relaxed in the warmth of her environment; I felt cared for and cared about without a word being said to that effect. Only after we had finished lunch and I was gathering up my coat and umbrella did she ask me, in the simplest manner, if she might pray for me.

Very few people have prayed for me in my presence, and they were friends who knew me well. I didn't know what to expect, but I said yes—not out of politeness, but out of some inner need I couldn't even express.

It was a short prayer, plainly spoken, but I think they may have been the most beautiful words I have ever heard. She asked Christ to share my sorrow—not to stop it; that would have demeaned the importance of my loss. She understood the true nature of my pain. *How?* So many people didn't—unless I told them, and I couldn't.

For a few moments I didn't speak, not because I was startled but because my placidity was shattered by the woman's love. I felt it more intensely than I have, at times, when the word *love* was mentioned. And that shattering was absolutely necessary for God to get to where the healing was needed.

That was a long time ago, and she and I know each

other better now. I also understand why she is able to sense, more than any other human being I know, when a person needs to be loved.

She has a son nearly my age who does not love her and who will not accept her love for him. It happens to many parents and their children; it begins with a conflict over values and life-styles, and it can end in bitter denunciations on both sides. I have known parents, good parents, who have thrown up their hands and decided that there was no way to love such children. I have listened to young men and women, good persons, recount how their parents no longer love them. I don't think that, in either case, there is no love. But there is no loving.

Not so with my friend. She goes on loving. Not out of habit. She has to be very innovative; she has to search hard for ways to love.

But not for reasons. She doesn't need them. Her love influences her thoughts, her emotions, her behavior, her perceptions. It motivates her relationships with others, not only part of the time, such as when she is with them or when her sentiments are touched by the events in their lives. She is loving all the time, and certainly in all relationships. To be in her presence is to feel her reverence for the God-created life in each of us.

She is not a doormat, and the reason I bring up the subject is that so many people are afraid to go on loving when their love is not wanted because they think it is humiliating. They forget that love doesn't always say yes, that it can object in very loud tones, that it can disagree, disapprove, and generally say exactly what is on its mind. They forget that Christ did not hesitate to speak in truth and in anger. Because to withhold such things is to withhold part of love itself. And if we limit ourselves to expressions of agreement—when there can be no agreement—then of course we find it almost impossible to love.

My friend is outspoken, and even then you can't miss the love in her voice. Or in her words. She never accuses; she never attacks; she never mistakes the behavior for the person. Yet she is accused and sometimes attacked in return, and it hurts her. The prolonged silences hurt even more, but they don't silence her. She keeps in touch, she writes, and she is overjoyed when the telephone rings, and, yes, it is her son calling. They do have moments of communication, and she has let it be known that she is there. Always. He does not have to negotiate when he is in need; he does not have to promise anything in return for help. He doesn't have to change, although lately he mentions that he is not happy with his life. He is not happy not loving.

She hopes. She has hoped before and probably always will. She has known disappointment many times. She can handle it. She says she keeps getting better at it.

We all know people who have stopped loving because they were hurt by the disappointment that may accompany it. But this woman's capacity to love has intensified and become more sensitive through her experiences of sadness as well as of joy. Giving has enabled her to give more. And, even knowing something of her pain, I can't feel sorry for her. I only hope I can become a little bit like her, whatever the cost. I only hope I can learn how to love—at least a little bit as well as she does. And if I do, then I hope someone will see in my eyes the caring that meant so much to me in a time of unutterable need.

I'm not describing a "silver lining." I'm not insisting that as bad as things are, we can find something good in them. Love isn't a consolation prize. It is the energy, the intelligence, and the creativity to deal with all of life, when it is bad and when it is good. It won't come up with a silver lining—but it will get you through darkness. Not always without injury. Not without pain. But alive. And fully a person.

If we are at all like Christ, or if we have learned anything from His life among us, then we cannot help but love. We will not always be understood, but it is imperative for us to understand that real love is not always acceptable to those we love—just as Christ was not always acceptable to those who clamored for Him. As He gave Himself on the cross in the hardest, most excruciating love, a sign over His head proclaimed it a joke.

There will be times when the love we give is returned with bitterness, even hate. Because it will not always be seen as love. If people cannot see what God has created in them, they may not accept what we see. In fact, they may attack our vision of them because they want to impose their own creation upon God's original. They may resent our love because it reminds them of what they do not want to become.

Don't take the attack personally. It will stun you. It will make you doubt your worth because, there you are, loving hard, and you're not being loved back. You're being rejected, possibly vilified, and you wonder if there might be any truth to the charges.

You can't know right away. You need some perspective. This time, instead of asking God to be close to you, step away from the situation and get close to God. Breathe His environment; measure yourself alongside the way Christ loves. If you measure up well, it doesn't change the fact that you've been wounded. And you need healing. You're in the right place for it. But if you have made mistakes, if you have been unfair and unloving, this is where you can learn what you don't yet know about love.

## When Do You Walk Away?

Someone asked me that recently. I didn't have the answer, but I knew someone who did.

Her name is Elizabeth, and because she is a warm, direct kind of person, everyone calls her Liz. I've known her for years. I've also wondered, for years, how she could put up with her sister Addy, short for Adelaide.

I always liked Liz. I did not like Addy. Liz was friendly and interested; Addy was hostile. When I was younger, I used to think Addy was difficult because she was ten years older than Liz and me and might have been annoyed by the behavior of children. Not so. Addy had problems. No one ever figured them out, but we couldn't help getting involved in them as time went on. Addy became an alcoholic.

When Liz and I were in high school, we used to sleep over at each other's houses. I didn't like being in Liz's house; we never knew when Addy would burst into the room and complain about something she accused Liz of doing earlier in the week. Did Liz use her comb? Did she hide some of her records? Why didn't she tell Addy that a friend had called?

Liz was very patient with her. She would look for missing articles, she would explain why no one would steal them, and eventually she would persuade Addy to go back to bed and get some sleep. Meanwhile, I would be pretending to be asleep with the covers pulled up over my head.

Everyone said Addy was "a little wild." But her problems ran deeper than that. She couldn't keep a job; twice she almost got married and then had mysterious reasons for deciding against it. She couldn't stay in one place, but she sent Liz cards from wherever she was because Liz collected postcards.

Liz's parents gave up on Addy, but Liz didn't. She never spoke as if she expected Addy to change, but she was always concerned about her. Even after she had a family of her own, she took the collect calls that came in the middle of the night and sat listening for as long as Addy wanted to talk.

I never knew whether Addy began to resent Liz for loving or whether alcoholism just makes people mean, but Addy began calling Liz more than once in a while. And more than once in the middle of the night. She didn't want comfort anymore; she wanted to blame Liz for her misery. Sometimes she didn't know what she wanted other than to wake Liz out of a sound sleep. There were other abuses, too. When Addy was in a drunken rage, she would call the police station in Liz's town and pretend that she was seriously ill; would they please contact her sister? At a birthday party for Liz's daughter, Addy showed up drunk and frightened the young guests by bursting the balloons strung across the dining-room ceiling. When Liz suggested that Addy seek professional care, Addy became hysterical. She broke things.

"I had no choice," Liz told me. "I had to get out of her reach." She arranged for an unlisted telephone number and finally got a good night's sleep. "Addy knows where I am," she explained. "She has my address. She knows I'll do anything I can to help her. She knows more than that—I love her."

It's still going on: the emergencies—some of them real and some false; the explanations to police and neighbors; the cost of repairing damages; the occasional admission to treatment centers and the vows that this time the cure will work; and the rapid denial of the vows once the treatment time is up.

"Why *don't* you walk away?" I asked Liz.

"From what?" she said. "From Addy?—or from love? I don't see where there's any difference. When you love, you love."

Sometimes it happens. We love someone who is so opposed to our love that we have to step aside from their attack. But we don't walk away. We remain in the vicinity. Waiting. Available. More than that: hoping.

It is very hard for love to stand at arm's length. Perhaps forever. It is easier to walk away and tell ourselves that someone isn't lovable. But it isn't true. Everyone is lovable; not everyone has learned how to love. This is something God had to confront—and so do we. We are left with alternatives similar to His: Do we decide when we will love? And under what conditions? Do we risk expressing this God-part of ourselves because it is as necessary to us as breathing? Or do we hold it back and lose it for lack of spiritual oxygen?

If I love you and you do not love me back, that has nothing to do with the color of my eyes or the nature of my being. I am still a loving person. And I have grown stronger in my ability to love by loving you. You cannot strengthen that ability by reciprocating it, however satisfying that would be. You can only strengthen your own ability to love by loving me back.

God is not made greater because we love Him; He uses His God-qualities by loving us. Christ was not able to do what He did for us because we loved Him—but because He loved us. It is our ability to love that gives us magnificence. It makes us who we are. This is what we get out of loving—even when it isn't easy.

*Why Do You Stay?*

There is a divinity in us and it is not meant to lie dormant until our life here is finished. The world has need of it; certainly we do. It is that part of God that does not give up on us, for He is a very stubborn lover of persons. So are we—if we don't limit ourselves to our human capabilities.

If you will think back to the times when you could no longer love someone, or someone could not love you—and if you are fiercely honest with yourself—I think you will realize that the greatest hurt of all was that *you* were prevented from loving as much as you believed you could. This is a terrible loss, not only to the one who will not accept love, but to the one who wants to give it. Much more than affection and endearment are thrust aside; much more than an important relationship is cut off; your ability to create each other is frustrated and you are incomplete. Your greatest need—to love—is left wanting. It is a form of spiritual isolation that only God can penetrate. And only your awareness of His love gives you the courage to emerge from it.

When you do, when you find yourself loving as a way of life, rather than as a way of response, you will achieve the freedom you have always sought. You will become your whole self. Your growth will not be stunted by disappointment, change, differences, or rejection; if anything, you will grow *through* them. When you are hurt, you will seek healing because you know it is possible.

And—while this may seem strange to you, but only at first—you will begin to understand that everything you are has meaning, because everything you are is of use. Not only in your life, but in the lives of others, many you may not even know by name. That is why we are here—and why we are created with such a tremendous need *to* love.